COOKING WITH TRADER JOE'S

Cookbook

SKINNY DISH!

Jennifer K. Reilly, RD

Cooking with Trader Joe's Cookbook: Skinny Dish!
by Jennifer K. Reilly, RD
Photographs by Jennifer K. Reilly, RD
Designed by Lilla Hangay
Produced by Deana Gunn and Wona Miniati

DISCLAIMER: The information in this book is not intended as medical advice nor intended to cure, treat, or diagnose any ailment or disease. The authors, publishers, and/or distributors do not assume responsibility for any adverse consequences resulting from adopting any health information or instructions described herein.

Published by Brown Bag Publishers, LLC
P.O. Box 235065
Encinitas, CA 92023
info@cookTJ.com

Printed in Korea through Overseas Printing Corporation

Library of Congress Cataloging-in-Publication Data
Reilly, Jennifer K., RD
Cooking with Trader Joe's Cookbook: Skinny Dish!/
by Jennifer K. Reilly, RD; photographs by Jennifer K. Reilly, RD – 1st ed.
Includes index.

I. Quick and easy cookery. 2. Trader Joe's (Store) I. Title.

ISBN   978-0-9799384-7-4
0-9799384-7-3

This book is an independent work not sponsored by or affiliated with Trader Joe's. Trader Joe's is a registered trademark of Trader Joe's Company.

Table of Contents

About the Author

Jennifer K. Reilly is a registered dietitian in Washington, D.C., crusading to make healthy eating hip, simple, fun, and scrumptious. Her passion for plant-based foods started in high school, after being told she'd be grounded if she became a vegetarian, and landed her in the front row of college nutrition lectures shortly thereafter. She earned a Bachelor of Science in Nutrition from Penn State and a registered dietetic degree from Virginia Tech. Following her college education, she became the managing director of The Cancer Project, a nonprofit organization dedicated to advancing cancer prevention and survival through nutrition education and research.

While at The Cancer Project, she developed the ***Food for Life: Nutrition & Cooking Class Series for Cancer Prevention and Survival,*** which focuses on cancer-related nutrition topics and corresponding cooking demonstrations. The ***Food for Life*** series is now taught in over 30 states nationwide. Jennifer co-authored ***The Cancer Survivor's Guide: Foods that help you fight back!*** with Dr. Neal Barnard. She was an expert panelist for ***Healthy Eating for Life***, a book series focused on nutrition for cancer, diabetes, children, and women's health. She has also helped write nutrition textbooks, video scripts, cookbooks, and has developed countless quick and easy healthy recipes.

Most recently, Jennifer has provided individual nutrition counseling, taught group nutrition sessions and cooking classes, and organized various educational activities at Discovery Communications, Inc., and the Nuclear Regulatory Commission. She writes a nutrition blog at BitchinDietitian.com, guest blogs and moderates forums on CrazySexyLife.com, and can be found on Twitter @DCdietitian. When she's not force-feeding people kale, beans, and quinoa, she is chasing after her three young children, vegetable gardening, and playing ultimate frisbee.

Foreword

By Kris Carr, author of *The New York Times* bestselling book, ***Crazy Sexy Diet***

How many different ways have you tried to get your weight under control and your energetic juices flowing? How many of those quick fix schemes have actually worked? Well, you're about to find a revolutionary plan that actually does work. Bitchin' Dietitian Jennifer Reilly has created an easy-breezy way for lifelong weight control that doesn't involve pills, shakes, or starvation. You'll feel more energized, empowered, and in control while following her brilliant tips and lip-smacking recipes. And she even makes her healthy plant-powered prescription fun as she walks you through metabolic-boosting guidelines and delicious power foods in "Skinny 101." You'll read, you'll cook, you'll eat, you'll laugh, you'll eat more, and then you'll get excited about all aspects of your magical new life.

Now I know you might be saying, "But change is hard, I don't have time, my family will revolt!" Regrouping and discovering new plant-powered foods and recipes can be overwhelming at first. For years, you've probably cycled through the same five dinners, and salads (or pretzels) and yogurt for lunch, only to find your healthy revolution continuously stuck in a rut. As a former actress and diet soda guzzler, I was in the same boat, but a cancer wake-up call forced me to get my act together overnight. Now, after swan diving into green juices and smoothies, beans, and lovely (and protein packed) grains like quinoa, I feel amazing and clear. My immune system is strong, and I'll never have to think about my weight again. Lucky for you, with Jen's simple, savory, and sweet recipes, she'll help you to shine at whatever pace you choose.

The eating plan is simple: come mealtime, load at least half your plate with yummy veggies (this book will make you crave them like a wild tiger), and the other half with the protein and whole-grain starchy foods you currently adore. Then, Jen will teach you how to get your protein priorities in order and reach for healthy beans, lentils, and nuts instead of chicken breast and lean ground beef, which are high in saturated fat and lack fiber and mighty antioxidants. Try this for three weeks and you'll be sold. No calorie counting, fear of fat grams, or magic pill needed. You have my Crazy Sexy word.

- *Kris Carr*

Introduction

Tired of "red light" diet books telling you what you can't eat, drink, or even look at if you want to stay slim and trim? Well, **Skinny Dish!** is just the opposite. It's not a diet book---it's a culinary green light suggesting dishes you can eat to your heart's content and still look smokin' hot. The more of these easy-to-prepare Trader Skinny dishes you devour, the healthier and more fabulous you'll look and feel. After all, what kind of red-light eating plan really works? You got it---none.

On this consumption journey, you'll learn to get cozy with vegetables, spices, beans, whole grains, and even chocolate (WHAT?!) as you reorient your dining mentality. Don't like veggies? Hate the texture of beans? Let Trader Skinny prove you wrong, and quickly! Healthy plant-stuffed cuisine need not take hours to prepare. Most of the recipes in this book take less than 30 minutes. Why? Because who has surplus time, especially when you have all that eating to do? For extra rushed nights, check out the **"Eight-Minute Meals"** section. Start with your eight-minute abs workout, and you'll have exercised and prepared dinner in less than 20 minutes!

For those who love cooking and spending time in the kitchen, don't fret. There are a handful of more involved Sunday-afternoon-type dishes, too. Getting back into the kitchen and putting some love labor into your food can certainly have its benefits.

In addition to all the glorious ways to *mangia, mangia, mangia*, you'll find tips on maximizing your metabolic machine, decoding nutrition labels, and making the most of your precious food dollar. Each recipe has nutrient analyses, gluten-free annotations, and heaps of alternate ingredient options.

For the folks who've caught the "detox" bug, or who've gotten a bug and need to detox, there's a whole section with guidelines and perfect recipes for following a mild, wellness-boosting detox. So without further ado, let's do this!

Skinny 101

How Skinny People Eat

Look around. What are the slim and trim folks eating? Fried chicken? Mayo-based macaroni salad? Maybe. But if that's the case, they're either eating small portions or large amounts of plant grub, too. Quite honestly, life's too short to limit any portion to a small one or to spend brain space worrying that a certain portion *should* be small. The only way to eat a lot and remain thin is to down more veggies and plant matter than you'd care to imagine. This plan is the complete package: eat large portions while lowering cholesterol, preventing diabetes, attaining "how does she do it?" energy levels, and most importantly, strutting a hot, slim body.

By choosing plant foods the majority of the time, it's a guarantee that you'll need to think even less about nutrient atoms and corpuscles, and will have more time to do what we're all here to do: EAT. Much of this has to do with boosting your metabolism (see **"Boosting Your Metabolism,"** page 14), but a lot of it just has to do with loading up on high-fiber foods, which also happen to be lower in fat and calories.

Why fiber? The Recommended Daily Intake is 25 grams per day. The average American gets about 11 grams per day, and, unfortunately, the average American is also squeezing into airline seats and buying seatbelt extenders. **How much fiber will keep you thin and trim and your cholesterol low? At least 40 grams per day**. For every 14 grams of fiber you eat, you'll consume about 10% fewer calories. As you increase your fiber intake, do so gradually to help your digestive system properly adapt. Fiber fills you up fast, keeps you full longer, and then shuttles all sorts of undesirables (toxins, cholesterol, unwanted hormones) out of your body. It's a wonder there's not a superhero named FiberMan. To see how easy it is to get 40 grams a day, see **"Sample Skinny Menu,"** page 22.

A fiber intake that will keep you thin: at least 40 grams per day.

A quick word about **Supplements:** The only nutrient naturally lacking in a completely plant-based diet is Vitamin B12. Regardless of diet, many folks are at risk for vitamin D deficiency. In addition, some women may need extra calcium, and some individuals may want to supplement with Omega-3 fatty acids because of a family history of heart disease. For these reasons, a daily multivitamin is recommended to meet vitamin B12 and vitamin D needs, and extra calcium and Omega 3's may be recommended as well.

The Five Rules of Skinny

1) Start Each Meal with a Tall Glass of Filtered Water.

However you take it: with a straw, ice, cucumber slices, a lemon wedge, or cayenne pepper (see **"When a Detox Knocks,"** page 28). Drinking plenty of water will ensure you're not just eating to quench your thirst. Water fills you up just like food does, and being properly hydrated will make you look 10 years younger.

2) Fill Half Your Plate with Veggies.

Without counting calories, fat molecules, or sugar particles, if you get in the habit of piling at least half your plate with veggies (a giant salad, a large size serving of roasted vegetables, or even steamed green beans with salt and pepper), you'll be on your way to simple slimdom.

As long as the veggies aren't slathered with butter and cheese sauce, they're likely to be loaded with filling fiber and life-powering nutrients. They are naturally low in calories, fat, saturated fat, and cholesterol. In fact, if you're really, really hungry, start your meal with a FULL plate of veggies, and then get to a second plate half covered with veggies. In no time, you'll be able to lift a car with a single finger.

3) Fill Half Your Plate with Whole Grains and Protein-Rich Plant Foods.

The other half of your plate is the protein-rich and starchy stuff—the stuff people who haven't read this book call the "good stuff." For guaranteed lifetime warranty slimdom, however, this half of your plate should include protein-rich plant foods like beans, lentils, tofu, tempeh, or veggie meats rather than meats and cheeses. Choose whole-grain starches like quinoa, brown rice, whole wheat pasta, a multigrain tortilla, or high-fiber bread over highly processed white carbs. Plant foods and whole grains fill you up faster and keep you full longer. They're lower in calories and fat, higher in fiber than their meaty, cheesy, and white bread counterparts, and don't leave you feeling zonked while your body tries to tear apart and make use of the dense, greasy, and sugary matter.

4) "What Does My Second Plate of Food Look Like?"

Very funny! The great news is that if you're choosing incredible foods like broccoli, tomatoes, beans, brown rice, whole grain tortillas, and recipes in this book, a second plate consisting of the half veggies, half grain and plant protein formula probably won't hurt you one bit. But before serving up *plat deux*, sit for a few minutes, and then try to be satisfied solely with additional portions of the vegetable matter. Proceed by checking out rule #5.

5) End Each Meal with Something Sweet.

A touch of something naturally sweet—especially something bittersweet—signifies the end of a meal for the satiety center of your brain. Once a little dark chocolate hits your palate, your stomach gets the signal that it's temporarily closed for business. Coffee (decaf especially if it's after noon) or tea often signifies break time just as well as sweets and chocolate. However, in my experience, a couple small pieces of dark chocolate, such as Fair Trade Swiss Dark Chocolate or Organic Dark Chocolate Truffle bar enjoyed slowly with eyes closed and ear plugs in, is quite heavenly. Then it's time to get back to non-food reality.

To see the **"The Five Rules of Skinny"** in action, jump to **"Sample Skinny Menu,"** page 20.

Boosting Your Metabolism

Rather than investing in useless pills, extracts, and empty promises, follow these six ways to safely and effectively rev up your inner engine. (Skinny people do all six.):

1) *Eat Frequently.* One of the best ways you can tell your metabolism to keep running
at its highest pace is to eat. When it thinks—even for a second—that the food supply is getting scarce, it slows down, and conserves fat. Very few people are in the market to conserve fat. So, unless you've just been dropped from a helicopter into the middle of the desert, or are lost mountaineering at 15,000 feet, set your inner alarm for meals and mini-meals every 2-3 hours. A day of constant eating looks something like this:

7:30 AM:	**Breakfast**
10:00 AM:	**Mini-Meal**
1:00 PM:	**Lunch**
4:00 PM:	**Mini-Meal**
7:00 PM:	**Dinner**
9:00 PM:	**Mini-Meal (but only if you're genuinely hungry)**

Eat Frequently. When your metabolism thinks— even for a second—that the food supply is getting scarce, it slows down and conserves fat.

Mini-meals? Snacks? What's the difference? Mini-meals are upgraded snacks. A bowl of pretzels is a snack, whereas a handful of whole grain pretzels and cucumber slices dipped in hummus is a mini-meal. Here are the 3 guidelines for meals and mini-meals:

A) Start each meal or mini-meal with a large glass (8+ ounces) of filtered water.

B) If you must count things, stick with 200-300 calories and 5+ grams of fiber for mini-meals, and 400-500 calories and 10+ grams of fiber for meals.

C) Always try for a utopian balance: a little protein, a touch of healthy fat (the kind that is liquid at room temperature), something whole grain and starchy, and a lot of something naturally colorful. (Sprinkles don't count).

Here are some real-life Mini-Meal Medleys.
While you read through these, isn't it about time for another feeding?

❀ Raw food bar (such as a Larabar®) + 1 tennis-ball-size serving of fruit
= 270 calories, 7 g fiber

❀ ¾ cup Crunchy Green Beans + ¼ cup Spicy Hummus = 290 calories, 8 g fiber

❀ ½ cup hummus such as *I ♥ Hummus* (page 71) + 20 Baked Lentil Chips
+ as many cucumber slices as you can handle = 210 calories, 10 g fiber

❀ 1 cup chopped raw veggies + 3 Tbsp dressing for dipping (such as Light Champagne
Vinaigrette)+ 15 wheat pretzels = 275 calories, 6 g fiber

❀ Homemade trail mix: ½ cup Multigrain O's cereal, ¼ cup raisins, 15 almonds,
1 tablespoon dark chocolate chips = 300 calories, 5 g fiber

❀ Half of a nut or seed butter banana sandwich: 1 Tbsp nut or seed butter
+ ½ banana + 1 slice high-fiber bread = 240 calories, 8 g fiber

❀ ¼ cup Fiberful Ends & Pieces + ¼ cup Pistachio Nutmeats = 240 calories, 9 g fiber

❀ Veggie Wrap: 1 whole grain or brown rice tortilla + 2 Tbsp bean spread
such as *Black Bean Dip* (page 86) + shredded veggies and lettuce = 250 calories, 10 g fiber

❀ 1 slice of vegetable-infused bread such as *Zucchini Bread* (page 208)
+ ½ cup raspberries = 250 calories, 8 g fiber

❀ 1 pkg Roasted Seaweed Snack + ¼ cup whole pecans = 260 calories, 5 g fiber

❀ 1 (6-oz) container peach soy yogurt stirred together with
1 cut-up organic peach = 220 calories, 5 g fiber

❀ 1 *Energy Bar* (page 230) + 3 sliced celery stalks
= 205 calories, 5 g fiber

2) Avoid Monstrous Meals.

This rule of metabolic boostocity is a close relative to eating frequently. Anytime you exceed your body's immediate needs for carbohydrate, protein, or fat, it stores the excess in your gut, buttocks, and that flabby chicken wing region of your upper arm. When it comes to protein, our bodies can really only handle about 20 grams at a time (the amount in a 3-oz chicken breast, which is the size of a deck of cards). This is one of the reasons why people downing veggies and beans—and skipping meats and cheeses—tend to be slimmer. A plant-based diet not only provides sufficient protein without any extra planning or steps, but it also avoids providing too much protein. Twenty grams of protein in beans would be about 1 ½ cups-worth. Can *you* eat that many?

3) Drink Tons of Filtered Water.

Not literally, though my recommended two liters for women and three liters for men may seem like tons. Without enough water, our kidneys don't work as well as they should. Our liver picks up the slack, leaving its stamina for burning fat less than ideal.

Just as our bodies slow down without enough food, a lack of water sends our systems into lost-in-the-woods survival mode, conserving and retaining fluid (in the form of kankles) and fat. Drink more water, mobilize your survival stores, and boost your fat-burning potential.

A lack of water sends our systems into survival mode, conserving fat and retaining fluid (in the form of kankles)

While straight-up, chilled, filtered water is best, caffeinated beverages (like coffee and tea) aren't totally useless as long as you're a regular offender. You actually get a decent amount of fluid from your daily cup o' Joe. However, if you have only occasional caffeinated beverages, your diuretic machine hasn't quite acclimatized and you'll only get about half the fluid toward your hydration goal du jour. Interestingly, green tea has been shown to boost your metabolism slightly and increase fat oxidation (a good thing). With the added bonus of its high antioxidant content, how about a cup o' green from time to time or a *Peachy Green Tea Smoothie* (page 47)?

Avoid diet sodas and artificial sweeteners. While diet beverages technically help you meet your fluid needs, fake sweeteners leave your body wondering why it didn't get any sugar out of the sweet-tasting beverage, causing you to eventually crave and scavenge for sugary treats. This disconnect abruptly halts your healthy renegade as you cycle through diet sodas, candy bars, guilt, more diet sodas, gummy worms, and so on.

4) Exercise and Build Muscle.
While it IS possible to maintain a healthy weight without exercise, moving your bod is a tremendous way to fire up your locomotive, sizzle away the flab, build a hot, toned body, and even increase your resting metabolism. The greater percent muscle you have, the faster your metabolism, even while watching brain-numbing reality TV. So, in addition to getting your heart rate up to a slightly uncomfortable place at least 3 times a week for 45 minutes, pump some iron about 3 times a week too. You're about to fill your pantry with towers of canned beans. Why not do some reps with them while watching your favorite show?

5) Eat a Plant-Heavy Diet.
Not only do fruits, veggies, beans, nuts, and whole grains have more butt-busting fiber and fewer calories compared to meatilicious and creamy foods, their thermic effect is higher than that of non-plant foods. This means your body heats up more to digest plant matter versus animal matter (almost as if you're exercising within your core). Plus, your resting metabolic rate is faster on a completely plant-based diet. It's as if your innards start sweating to an aerobics video the minute you eat plant foods, and then the video gets stuck on "repeat" as long as you continue to eat that way.

Your resting metabolic rate is faster on a completely plant-based diet.

6) Sleep. If you're typically running on empty sleep-wise, it's time for a heart-to-heart. With a good night's sleep (meaning 7+ hours, ideally when the sun is sleeping), you'll be able to choose healthier foods during the day, and your metabolic engine will be more cooperative.

Without adequate rest, your body is stressed, and responds by making more cortisol. This is GREAT if you're in the jungle running from a hungry tiger, but not if you're sitting in a PR planning meeting, or doing anything *other* than running from a hungry tiger. The stress hormone cortisol stimulates hunger and muddles up your ability to metabolize carbohydrates. In response, your blood sugar levels rise, which triggers insulin production and body fat storage. (NOT GOOD).

> *Without adequate rest, your body is stressed, and responds by making more cortisol, which stimulates hunger and stores body fat.*

Inadequate sleep also diminishes leptin levels, and leptin is something you want in mass quantities. Leptin triggers fullness and essentially tells your mouth that it's not taking any more customers. Without the right amount of leptin, you'll crave carbohydrates—not the kidney bean and quinoa type, but the twizzler-chocolately-marshmallow-fluff type. And you might be too tired to resist.

Finally, lack of sleep minimizes growth hormones that regulate fat and muscle proportions. (As you learned in #4, the more muscle you have, the faster your metabolism.) So, even if you're working out, you're going to have trouble building muscle. Just think: All that Zumba and nothing to show for it. Moreover, growth hormones are critical for graceful aging. A fat, saggy body topped off with extra wrinkles? No, thanks!

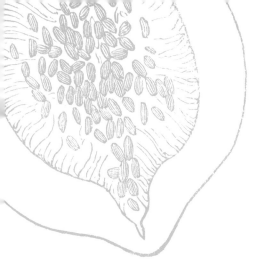

If you're having trouble falling asleep at night, or staying asleep, these tips have proven highly effective:

 Increase your protein intake at lunch to 20-25 grams (*Mediterranean Tofu Wrap*, page 150 plus *Carrot Ginger Soup*, page 94).

 Sip chamomile tea at bedtime and wind down with a good, boring book (hopefully not this one).

 Have a small, calming snack an hour before bedtime to include one or two foods rich in the sleepy hormone melatonin (tart cherries, bananas, tomatoes, oats, rice bran, sweet corn, wheatgrass juice, and ginger), or tryptophan (soy, almonds, peanuts, pumpkin seeds, spirulina, beans, and tofu).

 Take 1 mg supplemental melatonin an hour before bed with the approval of your doc.

 Exercise more, but not after 5:00 PM. Wear out your body so your mind can't ramp up when your head hits the pillow.

 Drink more water, but not all of it in the evening.

 Stop caffeine consumption at noon.

Sample Skinny Menu

Now it's time to put all these guidelines into action. You know you need to take in a small lake of water, piles of fiber, and gobs of vegetables every time you turn around, but how does that translate into tasty food? If you're skipping the meat, dairy, eggs, and Lemonheads, what's left? Wonder no more. The seven-day sample menu in this section demonstrates how these rules can transform brilliantly into grub you can get behind (with your behind in mind).

What About Calories?

You may notice that the daily calories in this sample are higher than other weight control plans. How can that be? Well, we all have different calorie needs for weight loss and weight maintenance, depending on current diet, starting weight, activity level, and goal weight. A diet built from supernatural plant foods overflowing with fiber and natural gems can be slightly higher in calories and still meet weight goals. The secret? Each gram of fiber accounts for four calories that your body is NOT depositing on your hips or wings. A diet built from these foods boosts your resting metabolism and the calorie-burning heat in your kiln (see **"Boosting Your Metabolism,"** page 14). Plus, varying your calorie intake from day to day tricks your metabolism and keeps it fresh and lively.

> *Varying your calorie intake from day to day keeps your metabolism in high gear, helping you burn calories more easily.*

If you're a numbers person and want to know what your exact calorie intake should be for weight loss, track your food intake on one typical work day and one typical non-work day while you're maintaining your weight. Enter those foods on a diet analysis site such as SparkPeople.com or Livestrong.com. The average of these two days is the number of daily calories you should consume for weight maintenance.

To lose weight, subtract 500 calories per day, which will give you a deficit of 3,500 calories per week and one pound of weight. So, if you're maintaining your weight at 2,300 calories per day, 1,800 calories would encourage one pound of weight loss per week, not accounting for any increase in exercise. You could also technically keep your food intake the same and exercise enough to burn an extra 500 calories per day. For most people, a combination of changing food habits and increasing exercise works best. Walking one mile burns about 100 calories. Walking one mile carrying armfuls of vegetables burns about twice that amount.

*The plan and food in **this** book are high in fiber and metabolic-boosting components, making calorie-counting unnecessary* for weight loss and weight maintenance. I've never met anyone who enjoys counting calories. Counting the number of pounds you've lost and number of days you HAVEN'T had to count calories, however, is highly enjoyable. Having said that, your own personal Skinny Menu may be somewhat higher or lower in calories than the following sample. Pay attention to your "hungry" and "full" cues, drink lots of water, load up on veggies, and you are going to rock this weight control thing once and for all.

A plant-based diet full of fiber can be higher in overall calories and still help you meet your weight goals.

In keeping with **"The Five Rules of Skinny,"** (page 12), start out each meal and mini-meal with a large (8-oz) glass of filtered water. Note that two sections of Organic Dark Chocolate Truffle bar or 20 g similar dark chocolate after lunch or dinner adds 90 calories and 2 g fiber. Also, coffee lovers (hi friends!) should add 30 calories and 0 g fiber for every 2 Tbsp Soy Milk Creamer they add to their morning brew.

Here is an example of one person's Skinny Menu, covering one week:

Each meal and mini-meal should be accompanied by a tall glass of filtered water.

One serving of each recipe unless otherwise indicated.

	Sunday 1769 calories 61 g fiber	**Monday** 1927 calories 59 g fiber	**Tuesday** 1615 calories 54 g fiber
Breakfast	2 *Confetti Pancakes* (p 65) with 2 Tbsp Organic Maple Agave Syrup Blend Organic apple	*Stick-With-You Oatmeal* (p 54) Navel orange	Shamrock Smoothie, incl. protein powder (p 38) 1 *Tater Shortcake* (p 53)
Mid–AM Mini-Meal	Cherry Pie Larabar® ½ cup blueberries	¼ cup Fiberful Ends & Pieces ¼ cup Pistachio Nutmeats	Nut butter banana sandwich made with: 1 Tbsp almond butter ½ banana 1 slice high-fiber bread
Lunch	*Lenticchie all'Arancia* (p 115) *Carrot Ginger Soup* (p 94)	*Mediterranean Tofu Wrap* (p150) *Gazpacho à la Shepherd Street* (p 97)	*Broccoli in a Blanket* (p 156) *Mango Summer Salad* (p 112)
Mid–PM Mini-Meal	1 pkg Roasted Seaweed Snack ¼ cup whole pecans	1 (6-oz) container peach soy yogurt 1 cut-up organic peach	1 slice *Zucchini Bread* (p 208) ½ cup raspberries
Dinner	*Loafin' Lentils* (p 170) *Garlicky Potatoes and Greens* (p 129) *Raspberry Applesauce* (p 220)	*Minute Mexican* (p 198) ½ cup *Guacamame* (p 83) with 2 sliced carrots	*Beijing Express* (p 192) 1 whole orange, cut into wedges

Wednesday	**Thursday**	**Friday**	**Saturday**
1968 calories 63 g fiber	1663 calories 53 g fiber	1801 calories 63 g fiber	1659 calories 47 g fiberr
Morning Quinoa (p 58) 2 kiwi fruits	2 slices multigrain bread 2 Tbsp sunflower seed butter 1 banana	3 *Breakfast Patties* (p 61) *Minty Fruit Salad* (p 226)	*Eggless Eggs* (p 62) *Mexican Potato Hash* (p 66)
1 (6-oz) container raspberry soy yogurt ½ cup blackberries	1 cup baby carrots 2 Tbsp White Bean Hummus 15 multigrain crackers	1 *Energy Bar* (p 230) 3 sliced celery stalks	Chocolate Brownie Pure Energy Bar® 6 organic strawberries
Lazy Lentils (p 196) 2 slices whole wheat baguette	*Tofu Feta, Walnut, and Beet Salad* (p 120) Whole wheat pita pocket	*Chicken Salad* (p 149) on high-fiber bread with lettuce & tomato 1 cup sugar snap peas	*Hot Chickpea Burger* (p 153) on a whole grain bun with sprouts and tomato slices
1 cup chopped raw veggies with 2 Tbsp *Fiery Cashew Dip* (p 76) 15 wheat pretzels	¾ cup Crunchy Green Beans ¼ cup Spicy Hummus	Veggie Wrap: 1 whole grain or brown rice tortilla + 2 Tbsp *Black Bean Dip* (p 86) ½ cup shredded veggies	*I ♥ Hummus* (p 71) 20 Baked Lentil Chips Cucumber slices
Broccoli Leek Soup (p 100) *Cannellini Ratatouille* (p 184) 2 *Squash Drop Cookies* (p 218)	*Chili Cook-Off* (p 188) *Hot Pants Cornbread* (p 229) Mixed greens salad with Light Champagne Vinaigrette	2 slices *Roasted Veggie Pizza* (p 182) *Blink-of-An-Eye Green Salad* (p 108) 4 slices cantaloupe	*The Big Tofu* (p 163) *Sesame Greens* (p 132) *Perfect Brown Rice* (p 234) 1 cup raspberries

Decoding Nutrition Labels

Does learning a foreign alphabet seem easier than figuring out nutrition labels? They have a wealth of information, but reading and decoding the nutrition information on food packages and at restaurants can put you in the loony bin. Does the 4,000 milligrams of sodium really matter? How about the 18 grams of sugar? Is that too much? Thankfully, I've developed **"The Under Over 10 Plan"** to help make the decoding much easier. With this plan, you only have to pay attention to two items, and you'll be on your way to a healthier, thinner, and more Zen you.

The Under Over 10 Plan

First: Look at the **Total Fat** grams. Each MEAL should ideally contain less than 10 grams of total fat (this is the *Under 10* part of the plan). When looking at individual labels that make up your meal make sure the total fat adds up to no more than 10 grams.

Second: Look at the **Dietary Fiber**. Each MEAL should ideally contain 10 or more grams of fiber (this is the *Over 10* part of the plan). Your fiber goal for the day is 40 grams. That breaks down to 10 grams for each of three meals and 5 grams for each of two snacks or mini-meals.

Let's test this out. You're at your favorite hang-out—Trader Joe's—and you've got this handy-dandy skinny guide with you. Which recipes fit in the plan? Trick question, of course! Take your pick. How about the *Sage White Bean Spaghetti* (page 191) with a side of *Green Beans with Rosemary Pecans and Cranberries* (page 139)? Sounds pretty healthy, but double-check it: 6.5 grams of Total Fat (Under 10), and 26.5 grams of Dietary Fiber (Over 10). Does it have a gazillion calories? Nope, just 453. Does it break the bank on saturated fat and cholesterol? Not even close: Just 1 gram of saturated fat and 0 milligrams of cholesterol.

Following the Under Over 10 Plan will guarantee that you're selecting foods low in calories, saturated fat, and cholesterol, moderate in sodium and sugar, and high in important disease-fighting nutrients. Many folks have been mistakenly following the OVER Under 10 Plan, which is not quite as successful!

Vitamin A, Vitamin C, Calcium, and Iron

On Nutrition Facts Panels and in this book, percents are provided for vitamin A, vitamin C, calcium, and iron. The percents are based on the following Recommended Daily Intakes:

Vitamin A: 5000 IU (International Units)
Vitamin C: 60 mg (milligrams)
Calcium: 1000 mg (milligrams)
Iron: 18 mg (milligrams)

For example, the *Sesame Greens* on page 132, have the following per serving:

113% Vitamin A = 5650 IU
99% Vitamin C = 59.4 mg
18% Calcium = 180 mg
13% Iron = 2.3 mg

Healthy Eating on the Cheap

The $1.99 Value Meal that includes a burger, fries, and a one-gallon soda seems pretty hard to beat when it comes to filling up fast on the cheap. Yes, the calorie-to-penny ratio is definitely a "good" one. When you start adding up the cost of organic baby eggplants and multi-grain bread, it's no wonder Ronald McDonald is a superstar. But guess who else is rising to stardom? Trader Joe! He's put the purse back in personality and made it possible to dine on a dime.

Here are some in-store and at-home tricks for making the most of your food pesos:

❀ *Plan Meals* and make a shopping list ahead of time.

❀ *Shop on a Full Stomach,* the best way to avoid those dangerous impulse buys.

❀ *Buy in Bulk.* Buy apples, potatoes, oranges, etc. by the bag rather than individually. Nuts, dried fruit, and grains are also more economical in large or bulk quantities.

❀ *Consider Frozen Produce.* Compare prices between fresh and frozen, and buy the cheaper. They're usually equally nutritious.

❀ *Go Meatless.* Eat as many meatless meals as possible using dried or canned beans for protein. Dried lentils go from dry to delish in just 30 minutes on low boil.

❀ *Make Vegetable Soup.* Use leftover rice or pasta, frozen veggies, tomato sauce, herbs, and beans to make a giant pot of vegetable soup. Freeze individual portions for lunches and snacks.

❀ *Buy Produce in Season,* and shred or chop and then freeze portions for later in the year. Shredded zucchini is more versatile than a Swiss Army Knife!

❀ *Sneak Veggies into Every Meal:* shredded in pancakes and muffins, and added to rice, pasta sauce, and mashed potatoes.

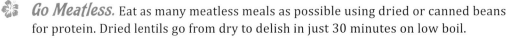

🌺 *Become a Scratch Cooker.* Make dips, hummus, breads, muffins, and pancakes from scratch, and freeze leftovers. It doesn't take that much longer, and you'll save some serious Yen.

🌺 *Drink Water,* filtered with your own filter. Spruce it up with sliced cucumbers, or lemon, lime, or orange wedges.

🌺 *Pack Your Lunch* and snacks for workdays using frozen leftovers, bulk foods, and produce.

🌺 *Organic* foods are best for about 62 reasons. However, they can be pricey. When it comes to produce, follow Environmental Working Group's lists for which ones should be organic (the "Dirty Dozen"), and the produce items lowest in pesticides (the "Clean 15")*. If you eat them, meat, dairy, and eggs should always be humanely-raised and organic.

*Dirty Dozen (Buy These Organic):
Celery, Peaches, Strawberries, Apples, Blueberries, Nectarines, Bell Peppers, Spinach, Cherries, Kale/Collard Greens, Potatoes, Imported Grapes.

*Clean 15 (Lowest in Pesticides):
Onions, Avocado, Sweet Corn, Pineapple, Mangos, Sweet Peas, Asparagus, Kiwi, Cabbage, Eggplant, Cantaloupe, Watermelon, Grapefruit, Sweet Potatoes, Honeydew Melon.

Source: Environmental Working Group, 2010, www.FoodNews.org

When a Detox Knocks

Having trouble focusing, motivating, or energizing? Are you a hot mess? Do you need to jumpstart your weight loss plan or boost your wellness? Maybe you need recovery from too much Saturday night. A mild detox to the rescue! Eating a mostly raw, easy-on-the-system detoxification diet one day a week, three days every other week, or seven days a month can be a great way to de-gum your system and get you living life with more spirit, passion, and health-boosting supremacy. Luckily for you, many of the recipes in this book fit beautifully into a mild detox plan.

Why Do a Detox?

Day after day we take in unwanted and unhealthy toxins in our food, water, and air supply. These villains get stored in our fat cells, and it's next to impossible to avoid them completely. They're pesticides, mold byproducts, antibiotics, hormones, food additives and preservatives, chemicals in food packaging, household cleaners, heavy metals, car exhaust and other air pollutants, and cigarette smoke. Our body's natural detoxification system does a decent job of eliminating some of these, but can't deal with all the toxins present in our modern world. Moreover, a shabby diet lacks certain vital nutrients to naturally detox, leading to further buildup in the body.

Such buildup is responsible for a crummy immune system, nutritional deficiencies, hormonal imbalances, and a poorly oiled metabolic machine. Real life signs of this buildup include indigestion, poor attention span, fatigue, stinky breath, acne and other skin problems, low sex drive, headaches, food cravings, muscle pain, and weight changes.

Following a mild detox 1 day a week, 3 days every other week, or 7 days a month can improve your digestion, skin clarity, energy levels, and ability to concentrate, while also promoting more restful sleep, regular bowel movements, fewer unhealthy food cravings, and a speedier metabolism.

A mild detox pumps up your energy and metabolism, while it clears up your mind and your skin.

Pregnant and nursing women, children, and folks with chronic diseases can certainly include the foods indicated in a mild detox in their every day, but should only do frequent or regular detoxes with blessings from their doc.

Detox Preparation

Follow these guidelines for the 3 days leading up to the detox:

1) Phase out caffeine.

2) Limit portions of meat, dairy, eggs, gluten (wheat), and alcohol to no more than 1 serving of each per day.

3) Grocery shop.

4) Completely ditch processed sugar and refined carbohydrates (use agave nectar & stevia to sweeten foods).

5) Increase your intake of vegetables and filtered water.

6) Clean off your appliances (blender/juicer) and take them out for a test drive.

Detox Guidelines

1) Start the day with a large glass of filtered water with lemon or cucumber slices. Add a dash of cayenne for an extra kick in the pants.

2) Consume only liquids (green juices, non-dairy smoothies, herbal tea, filtered water) and raw fruits and veggies until noon every day.

3) Drink tons of filtered water throughout the day, at least half your body weight in ounces (150 lbs: drink 75 oz. water). No sense in detoxing if the crud can't ride the river out.

4) Eat lots of raw fruits and veggies, preferably organic. The more the better. Allow some raw nuts and seeds (about ½ cup each day) and cooked whole grains (about 2 cups total) spread out throughout the afternoon, but avoid gluten (wheat, barley, rye) completely.

5) At least 80% of your diet should be comprised of raw foods, and 20% can be cooked grains, beans, and vegetables.

6) Include a daily multivitamin to ensure adequate vitamin B12 and vitamin D intake.

7) Avoid all dairy products, meats, fish, sugar, gluten, alcohol, and caffeine.

8) Add more green juices and raw foods as needed for energy. Larger servings of grains and nuts can also be added for more fuel if needed.

9) Substitute different nuts, seeds, or legumes for allergenic foods.

10) Expect a headache for the first couple days. But, if you feel extra crummy (beyond a headache), add larger servings of foods within the guidelines or stop the detox and begin again once you've done a few more days of Detox Prep.

Here are 7 sample detox days. Do all 7 days in a row each month or choose 1 or 3 of the sample days to do every week or every other week. You can even get creative and invent your own day using the Detox Guidelines.

Detox Day 1

Upon Waking *(7:00 AM)*
Large glass of filtered water with cucumber slices and a dash of cayenne

Breakfast *(8:00 AM)*
Green-Apple Juice (Serves 1):
JUICER: Use organic ingredients if possible: 2 kale leaves, handful spinach, 1 stalk celery, small handful parsley, and 2 tart apples. Serve over ice. BLENDER: Same recipe, but add 4-8 ounces water and a handful of ice.

Morning Snack *(10:00 AM)*
Herbal tea, 1 cup raspberries

1 Hour Later *(11:00 AM)*
Large glass of filtered water with cucumber slices

Lunch *(12:00 PM)*
Mango Summer Salad (page 112)
1 cup brown rice

Mid-Afternoon Snack *(2:00 PM)*
Large glass of filtered water with lemon wedge
I ♥ *Hummus* (page 71) with sliced veggies

Pre-Dinner Snack *(4:00 PM)*
Herbal tea; 15 raw almonds

Dinner *(6:00 PM)*
3 cups lightly steamed broccoli
½ cup quinoa
½ cup lentils
Filtered water

Before Bed *(8:00 PM)*
Chamomile or other herbal tea

Detox Day 2

Upon Waking *(7:00 AM)*
Large glass of filtered water with cucumber slices and a dash of cayenne

Breakfast *(8:00 AM)*
Carrot Orange Cucumber Shake (page 48)

Morning Snack *(10:00 AM)*
Herbal tea
1 cup blueberries

1 Hour Later *(11:00 AM)*
Large glass of filtered water with cucumber slices

Lunch *(12:00 PM)*
8-10 pieces of veggie sushi rolls wrapped in nori with rice (cucumber, carrot, avocado, etc.)

Mid-Afternoon Snack *(2:00 PM)*
Large glass of filtered water with lemon wedge
Sliced veggies dipped in Goddess Dressing

Pre-Dinner Snack *(4:00 PM)*
Herbal tea
¼ cup raw cashews

Dinner *(6:00 PM)*
Carrot Ginger Soup (page 94)
Rice crackers
¼ cup sunflower seeds

Before Bed *(8:00 PM)*
Chamomile or other herbal tea

Detox Day 3

Upon Waking *(7:00 AM)*
Large glass of filtered water with cucumber slices and a dash of cayenne

Breakfast *(8:00 AM)*
Shamrock Smoothie (page 38)

Morning Snack *(10:00 AM)*
Herbal tea, large dish of sliced strawberries

1 Hour Later *(11:00 AM)*
Large glass of filtered water with cucumber slices

Lunch *(12:00 PM)*
Gigantic green salad (as many veggies as you'd like) topped with ½ cup kidney beans
1 cup brown rice
Filtered water

Mid-Afternoon Snack *(2:00 PM)*
Large glass of filtered water with lemon wedge
Organic apple slices dipped in almond butter

Pre-Dinner Snack *(4:00 PM)*
Herbal tea
¼ cup walnuts

Dinner *(6:00 PM)*
Veggie Pupusas (page 155)

Before Bed *(8:00 PM)*
Chamomile or other herbal tea

Detox Day 4

Upon Waking *(7:00 AM)*
Large glass of filtered water with cucumber slices and a dash of cayenne

Breakfast *(8:00 AM)*
Purple Nurple (page 44)

Morning Snack *(10:00 AM)*
Herbal tea
2 fresh pears

1 Hour Later *(11:00 AM)*
Large glass of filtered water with cucumber slices

Lunch *(12:00 PM)*
Tofu Feta, Walnut, and Beet Salad (page 120)
Gluten-free crackers

Mid-Afternoon Snack *(2:00 PM)*
Large glass of filtered water with lemon wedge
Black Bean Dip (page 87) with sliced veggies

Pre-Dinner Snack *(4:00 PM)*
Herbal tea
15 raw almonds

Dinner *(6:00 PM)*
Curried Lentil Stew (page 98)
1 cup cooked quinoa

Before Bed *(8:00 PM)*
Chamomile or other herbal tea

Detox Day 5

Upon Waking *(7:00 AM)*
Large glass of filtered water with cucumber slices and a dash of cayenne

Breakfast *(8:00 AM)*
Decaf *Peachy Green Tea Smoothie* (page 47)

Morning Snack *(10:00 AM)*
Herbal tea
1 organic green apple

1 Hour Later *(11:00 AM)*
Large glass of filtered water with cucumber slices

Lunch *(12:00 PM)*
Kaleidoscope Bean Salad (page 116)

Mid-Afternoon Snack *(2:00 PM)*
Large glass of filtered water with lemon wedge
Carrot slices with Goddess Dressing

Pre-Dinner Snack *(4:00 PM)*
Herbal tea
¼ cup cashews

Dinner *(6:00 PM)*
Large green salad with veggies of choice, sliced tempeh cubes, and rice vinegar
1 cup cooked brown rice

Before Bed *(8:00 PM)*
Chamomile or other herbal tea

Detox Day 6

Upon Waking *(7:00 AM)*
Large glass of filtered water with cucumber slices and a dash of cayenne

Breakfast *(8:00 AM)*
Mango Lassi (page 43)

Morning Snack *(10:00 AM)*
Herbal tea
1 cup blackberries

1 Hour Later *(11:00 AM)*
Large glass of filtered water with lemon slices

Lunch *(12:00 PM)*
Sesame Greens (page 132)
½ cup black beans
1 cup corn

Mid-Afternoon Snack *(2:00 PM)*
Large glass of filtered water with lemon wedge
Organic celery slices and *Fiery Cashew Dip* (page 77)

Pre-Dinner Snack *(4:00 PM)*
Herbal tea
15 raw almonds

Dinner *(6:00 PM)*
Garden Grower's Special (page 118)
Guacamame (page 83) with corn chips

Before Bed *(8:00 PM)*
Chamomile or other herbal tea

Detox Day 7

Upon Waking *(7:00 AM)*
Large glass of filtered water with cucumber
slices and a dash of cayenne

Breakfast *(8:00 AM)*
Carrot Orange Cucumber Shake (page 48)

Morning Snack *(10:00 AM)*
Herbal tea
1 cup raspberries

1 Hour Later *(11:00 AM)*
Large glass of filtered water with
cucumber slices

Lunch *(12:00 PM)*
*Arugula Salad with Pan-Seared
Butternut Squash* (page 111)
¼ cup pistachios

Mid-Afternoon Snack *(2:00 PM)*
Large glass of filtered water with lemon wedge
Gluten-free crackers
Almond butter

Pre-Dinner Snack *(4:00 PM)*
Herbal tea
1 organic green apple

Dinner *(6:00 PM)*
Curried Sweet Potato Soup (page 105)
1 cup quinoa

Before Bed *(8:00 PM)*
Chamomile or other herbal tea

About the Recipes

Each recipe in this book contains ingredients that can be found at Trader Joe's. While many of the ingredients are generic, ingredients that are capitalized are specific products found at Trader Joe's.

Each recipe includes prep time and cooking time. For those dishes that are assembled and then simmer on the stove or bake in the oven, I indicate "hands-off cooking time." Take this time to relax or catch up on other work.

Each recipe contains nutritional data. Optional ingredients are not included when calculating nutritional data. Serving sizes follow FDA guidelines and my recommendations.

Each recipe contains indicators for recipes that are **gluten-free**. Please note that the FDA has not established a standard to define the term gluten-free. Products at Trader Joe's may be labeled "no gluten ingredients used" which does not necessarily exclude the chance of cross-contamination if it is produced in a facility that handles gluten products. Persons with celiac disease or severe gluten allergies should note that unless a product is labeled and tested gluten-free by standards such as ELISA and produced in a dedicated facility, there is possibility of cross-contamination.

Gluten-Free

G
Gluten Free

The Recipes

Liquid Skinny

Shamrock Smoothie

You know it's going to be a good day when you get a serving of vegetables at breakfast. This green machine is not only naturally sweet, delicious, and a favorite among kids, but the raw greens and Very Green powder pack a powerful chlorophyll punch. Chlorophyll is a cleansing and purifying agent, and it helps relieve congestion, lower high blood pressure, strengthen blood, and even increases energy levels. Sold? Add ¼ cup protein powder (such as Organic Hemp Protein Powder, Vanilla Flavored) for an extra 4.5 grams of protein, 5.5 grams fiber, and 65 calories per serving.

1 banana

1 cup frozen Pineapple Tidbits

1 cup frozen Mango Chunks (about 14 pieces)

½ cup green grapes (preferably organic)

2 Tbsp orange juice concentrate (not reconstituted)

1 Tbsp Very Green Dietary Supplement, or other green superfood powder (optional)

1 large handful (about 1 cup) raw baby spinach or kale (preferably organic)

2 cups unsweetened almond milk

1 Blend all ingredients together until smooth. Cheers!

2 Leftovers will not keep very well in the fridge. Pour leftovers into popsicle molds for a delicious frozen treat.

Nutrition Snapshot
Per serving: 114 calories, 2 g total fat, 0 g saturated fat, 0 mg cholesterol, 101 mg sodium, 25 g carbohydrates, 3 g fiber, 15 g sugar, 2 g protein, 27% vitamin A, 44% vitamin C, 13% calcium, 7% iron

G Gluten Free

Makes 4 (1-cup) servings
Prep time 5 minutes

The 5 AM Latte

This latte was born during a period of early mornings and overdrive days. After drinking it, you'll look outside and say to yourself, "The sun's not up yet? What's it waiting for?" Vanilla almond milk is creamy and sweet, so you needn't add sugar. If you have an espresso machine, get the stepladder, dust it off, and fire it up. If not, brew double-strength coffee and this'll be just as fierce.

1 cup (8 oz) vanilla almond milk

Dash cinnamon

2 shots of brewed espresso such as Organic Fair Trade Five Country Espresso Blend, or 2 oz brewed double-strength dark roast coffee such as Bay Blend

1 Microwave or heat milk and cinnamon in a saucepan until steamy hot (about 1 minute in most microwaves). Pour it into your favorite mug.

2 Brew coffee or espresso and pour immediately into the mug o' milk. Sip fast or slow. Let the day begin!

Nutrition Snapshot
Per serving: 93 calories, 2.5 g total fat, 0 g saturated fat, 0 mg cholesterol, 152 mg sodium, 16.5 g carbohydrates, 1.5 g fiber, 15 g sugar, 1 g protein, 10% vitamin A, 0.5% vitamin C, 21% calcium, 3.5% iron

G Gluten Free

Serves 1
Prep time 5 minutes

Mango Lassi

Have this beta-carotene-rich drink for breakfast, a snack, or an after-meal treat. Antioxidants never tasted so good!

1 cup frozen Mango Chunks (about 14 pieces), or 1 mango, cut into chunks, plus 1 cup ice

1 Tbsp orange juice concentrate (not reconstituted)

1 tsp vanilla

2 cups (16 oz) almond, soy, or other non-dairy milk

Dash ground cardamom or nutmeg (optional)

1 Blend all ingredients except ground cardamom or nutmeg together until creamy.

2 Pour into glasses and top each one with cardamom or nutmeg, if using.

3 Store leftovers in the fridge for up to 1 day (may need to re-blend), or pour leftovers into popsicle molds for a delicious frozen treat.

Nutrition Snapshot
Per serving: 113 calories, 1.5 g total fat, 0 g saturated fat, 0 mg cholesterol, 100 mg sodium, 21.5 g carbohydrates, 2 g fiber, 15.5 g sugar, 1.5 g protein, 23.5% vitamin A, 28.5% vitamin C, 13.5% calcium, 5.5% iron

Gluten Free

Makes 3 (1-cup) servings
Prep time 5 minutes

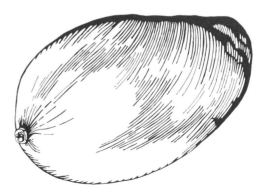

Purple Nurple

The deep color of blackberries, blueberries, and raspberries is thanks to their high anthocyanin content—the antioxidant that helps lower cancer risk, improve urinary tract health, memory function, and promote healthy aging. These berries also have ellagic acid—another tough anti-viral, anti-bacterial, and anti-cancer compound getting a name for itself in the area of tumor reversal. Need a wicked awesome way to get these powerhouses into your being? Search no more!

2 cups frozen Fancy Berry Medley, or other frozen berry mix
2 cups (16 oz) organic original soy milk, or other non-dairy milk
1 cup filtered water
3 Tbsp orange juice concentrate (not reconstituted)

1 Blend ingredients together until smooth. For a thinner smoothie, add more water, ¼ cup at a time.

2 Store leftovers in the fridge for up to 1 day (may need to re-blend), or pour leftovers into popsicle molds for a delicious frozen treat.

Nutrition Snapshot
Per serving: 99 calories, 2 g total fat, 0.5 g saturated fat, 0 mg cholesterol, 35 mg sodium, 16 g carbohydrates, 3 g fiber, 12 g sugar, 5 g protein, 5.5% vitamin A, 26.5% vitamin C, 16% calcium, 9% iron

G
Gluten Free

Makes 4 (1-cup) servings
Prep time 5 minutes

Peachy Green Tea Smoothie

Green tea is loaded with immune-boosting antioxidants, and regular consumption may even increase your metabolism. A chilled smoothie is a refreshing way to get your tea on, and is especially handy during summer months when hot tea is the farthest thing from your mind.

1 (8-oz) cup brewed double-strength (2 tea bags) green tea, or decaf green tea
2 cups ice cubes
2 peaches, unpeeled, pit removed (preferably organic), or 4 Yellow Cling Peach Halves
1 banana

1 Blend ingredients together until smooth. For a thicker smoothie, add more ice, a handful of cubes at a time.

2 Leftovers will not keep very well in the fridge. Go share with a neighbor.

Nutrition Snapshot
Per serving: 48 calories, 0 g total fat, 0 g saturated fat, 0 mg cholesterol, 0 mg sodium, 12.5 g carbohydrates, 1.5 g fiber, 3.5 g sugar, 0.5 g protein, 5.5% vitamin A, 10% vitamin C, 0.5% calcium, 1% iron

Gluten Free

Makes 4 (1-cup) servings
Prep time 5 minutes

Carrot Orange Cucumber Shake

Too busy to chew your veggies? Let your blender do the work. This nutrient-heavy combination includes ginger, which eases digestion, calms your appetite, and makes you feel tingly all over. Feel great getting more than a day's recommended supply of vitamin A in one cup!

3 carrots, scrubbed, unpeeled, and cut into large chunks
½ organic cucumber, unpeeled
2 oranges, peeled
½-inch round piece ginger, peeled*
1 cup chilled filtered water
10 ice cubes (a handful)

1 Blend ingredients together until smooth. For a thicker smoothie, add more ice cubes, a handful at a time. For a thinner smoothie, add more chilled filtered water, ¼ cup at a time.

2 Store leftovers in the fridge for up to 24 hours. Or, pour leftovers into popsicle molds for a delicious frozen treat.

Nutrition Snapshot

Per serving: 47 calories, 0 g total fat, 0 g saturated fat, 0 mg cholesterol, 32 mg sodium, 11 g carbohydrates, 2.5 g fiber, 6.5 g sugar, 1 g protein, 113.5% vitamin A, 50.5% vitamin C, 4% calcium, 1.5% iron

*Tip Fresh ginger root can easily and safely be peeled by using the edge of a metal teaspoon. You'll get over the root's bumps and lumps without wasting any prime ginger.

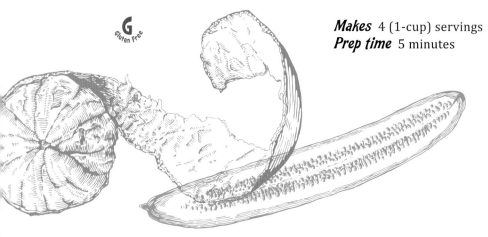

G
Gluten Free

Makes 4 (1-cup) servings
Prep time 5 minutes

Rise & Shine

Tater Shortcakes

These plump orange masterpieces are a quick and nutritious way to start the day. Use yams, sweet potatoes, or even canned pumpkin to maximize the beta-carotene kick (although pumpkin is actually a squash, thus making these "squashcakes." Yum!)

1 medium yam or sweet potato, peeling optional, cut into chunks plus ½ cup water, or 1 (15-oz) can pumpkin purée

2 cups whole wheat flour

1 Tbsp baking powder

¾ cup vanilla almond milk or other non-dairy milk

2 tsp cinnamon

1 tsp ginger

½ tsp nutmeg

½ tsp ground cloves

½ cup unsweetened applesauce

2 Tbsp sugar

½ cup dried cranberries or raisins

1 Preheat oven to 400° F.

2 In a medium-sized pot, cook chunked yam or sweet potato in ½ cup water over medium-high heat, covered, until soft, about 10 minutes.

3 Combine remaining ingredients. Blend or mash yam or sweet potato with cooking water and add to the batter. (If using pumpkin purée, simply stir it into the batter without heating or adding any water.)

4 On a lightly greased baking sheet, drop large spoonfuls 1-2 inches apart. For flatter shortcakes, gently press down on each dropped spoonful with the backside of a spoon. Bake for 12 minutes, or until lightly browned. Serve warm.

5 Shortcakes are best eaten fresh out of the oven, but can be stored in zipper sealed bags for up to 2 days. Leftovers can be frozen for up to 3 months, and reheated in the microwave or toaster oven as needed.

Nutrition Snapshot
Per shortcake: 90 calories, 0.5 g total fat, 0 g saturated fat, 0 mg cholesterol, 131 mg sodium, 19 g carbohydrates, 2 g fiber, 6 g sugar, 2 g protein, 34% vitamin A, 5.5% vitamin C, 8% calcium, 4% iron

Makes 16 shortcakes
Prep time 15 minutes
Hands-off cooking time
15 minutes

Stick-With-You Oatmeal

While instant oatmeal packets are quick and easy, they tend to give very short-term satisfaction. This oatmeal has a near-instant preparation and it will keep you chugging through all your morning activities with energy and a smile. A hearty dose of cinnamon helps control blood sugar levels, keeping you even-keeled all morning long.

½ cup old-fashioned rolled oats

1 tsp cinnamon

1 small organic gala or Fuji apple, cored and diced (unpeeled)

¼ cup cashews, crushed or left whole

1 cup filtered water

¼ cup vanilla almond, rice, or soy milk

1 Combine all ingredients except non-dairy milk in a microwave-safe bowl and microwave for 2 minutes.

2 Add non-dairy milk, stir, enjoy, and go!

Nutrition Snapshot
Per serving: 392 calories, 16.6 g total fat, 2.5 g saturated fat, 0 mg cholesterol, 127 mg sodium, 56.5 g carbohydrates, 8 g fiber, 18.5 g sugar, 9.5 g protein, 2.5% vitamin A, 0% vitamin C, 9% calcium, 20.5% iron

G
Gluten Free
Use oats tested for gluten, or use ¾ cup cooked quinoa in place of oats

Makes 1 serving
Prep and cooking time 7 minutes

French Toast for Gods and Goddesses

Traditional French toast can be loaded with calories, saturated fat, and cholesterol, weighing you down as you're taking names and organizing galaxies. Enjoy this cholesterol-free, lower-calorie version, and rule the universe with grace and ease. This recipe uses grapeseed oil for pan-frying because it has a high smoke point—meaning it takes a lot of heat for it to burn. You will add less oil and fewer calories to get the same crispy toast effect.

1 ¼ cups (10 oz) vanilla soy milk, or other non-dairy milk
2 Tbsp flour
2 Tbsp flaxseed meal (ground flaxseeds), or Just Almond Meal
2 tsp cinnamon
2 tsp sugar
3 Tbsp grapeseed oil
6 slices of whole wheat bread

1 Whisk milk, flour, flaxseed meal, cinnamon, and sugar together in a mixing bowl until well-mixed. Pour into a pie dish, or 9-inch square or round baking pan.

2 Heat oil in a large skillet over medium-high heat. Dip each slice of bread into the milk mixture on both sides and place in the skillet. Reduce heat to low, and cook until golden brown, about 20 minutes total, flipping every few minutes to prevent sticking.

3 Serve with pure maple syrup, agave nectar, powdered sugar, or nothing at all.

4 French Toast should be eaten immediately or can be frozen for up to 2 months and toasted for a quick breakfast or snack any time.

Nutrition Snapshot
Per slice: 195 calories, 10 g total fat, 0.5 g saturated fat, 0 mg cholesterol, 150 mg sodium, 21 g carbohydrates, 3 g fiber, 4 g sugar, 6 g protein, 2% vitamin A, 0% vitamin C, 10.5% calcium, 6% iron

Note Make your own flaxseed meal by grinding flaxseeds in a coffee bean grinder.

G Gluten Free Use gluten-free bread and almond meal in place of flour

Makes 6 slices (about 3 servings)
Prep and cooking time 30 minutes

Morning Quinoa

A twist on oatmeal, this gluten-free hot cereal is high in protein, fiber, and iron, and will keep you energized all morning long. Make this breakfast with the previous night's 2 cups of leftover cooked quinoa, and reduce the prep and cooking time by 15 minutes.

½ cup quinoa, rinsed vigorously in cold water and then drained

1 ½ cups filtered water

½ tsp cinnamon

¼ cup vanilla almond milk, or other non-dairy milk

5 California Slab Apricots, or other dried apricots, chopped

2 Tbsp raisins (packed into measuring spoon)

1 Tbsp Organic Raw Blue Agave, or other agave nectar or maple syrup

1 In a medium dry saucepan, toast rinsed quinoa over medium-high heat for 2 minutes, until it starts to crackle.

2 Add water and cinnamon, bring to a boil; continue to cook for 12 minutes, until all water is absorbed.

3 Stir in almond milk, apricots, raisins, and agave; continue to cook for 1-2 minutes. Remove from heat and serve.

4 Leftovers will last in the fridge for up to 3 days—reheat and go!

Nutrition Snapshot
Per serving: 272 calories, 3 g total fat, 0 g saturated fat, 0 mg cholesterol, 21 mg sodium, 55.5 g carbohydrates, 4 g fiber, 23 g sugar, 7 g protein, 6.5% vitamin A, 3% vitamin C, 3.5% calcium, 15.5% iron

Note Rinsing quinoa removes saponins, which are slightly bitter. Some varieties of quinoa are pre-rinsed, as noted on their package.

G Gluten Free

Makes 2 servings
Prep and cooking time 20 minutes

Cooking with Trader Joe's Cookbook *Skinny Dish!* **CookTJ.com**

Breakfast Patties

Are you in the habit of a sausage-style power breakfast, or do you just need more than a bowl of cereal to kick it into gear in the morning? Well, these patties—adapted from a recipe by Kristin Doyle, Registered Nurse and therapeutic chef in San Francisco, California—are for you. Enjoy them with whole grain bread, Eggless Eggs (page 62), and fresh fruit. Make a double or triple batch and freeze them for rush-out-the-door days. They can be formed into meatballs instead of patties for a delish lunch or dinner. Don't be intimidated by the list of ingredients—most of them are spices you already have in your arsenal.

2 Tbsp flaxseed meal (ground flaxseeds), soaked in ¼ cup warm water for 10 minutes to form a gel, or 2 Tbsp cornstarch dissolved in ¼ cup warm water

1 (8-oz) pkg Organic 3 Grain Tempeh, broken into chunks and boiled for 8 minutes

1 tsp ground cumin

1 tsp onion powder

1 tsp garlic powder

½ tsp dried sage, or 1 Tbsp chopped fresh sage

½ tsp dried thyme

⅛ tsp cayenne pepper

1 Tbsp whole grain flour, such as whole wheat flour

1 Tbsp Organic Raw Blue Agave, or other agave nectar or maple syrup

1 Tbsp olive oil

1 Tbsp reduced-sodium soy sauce

1 Preheat oven to 350° F.

2 In a medium-sized saucepan, cover tempeh chunks with water and bring to a boil for 8 minutes.

3 Meanwhile, combine spices and flour in a medium-sized mixing bowl. Add agave, oil, soy sauce and gelled flaxseed meal.

4 Drain tempeh and add it to mixing bowl. Using a fork or potato masher, mix thoroughly.

5 Form patties and place on baking sheet lined with parchment paper. Bake for 20 minutes. Flip and bake another 5 minutes.

6 Store leftovers in the fridge for 3 days or in the freezer for up to 2 months.

Nutrition Snapshot

Per patty: 76 calories, 4 g total fat, 0.5 g saturated fat, 0 mg cholesterol, 48 mg sodium, 6 g carbohydrates, 2.5 g fiber, 1.5 g sugar, 4.5 g protein, 0% vitamin A, 0% vitamin C, 2% calcium, 3.5% iron

Makes 10 patties
Prep time 20 minutes
Hands–off cooking time 25 minutes

Eggless Eggs

Searching for scrambled eggs without all the fat and cholesterol? Take this creation out for a spin, and you'll find yourself singing its praises from the hilltops. Serve with fresh fruit and toasted multigrain bread. Compared to a 2-egg omelet, a serving of Eggless Eggs has 150 fewer calories, 11 fewer grams of fat, 450 fewer milligrams of cholesterol, and 2 more grams of fiber. Eggs never tasted so good.

1 (15-oz) block extra firm tofu
2 tsp olive oil
1 Tbsp diced onion
½ red bell pepper, diced (preferably organic)
½ green bell pepper, diced (preferably organic)
1 medium carrot, diced
½ tsp garlic powder
½ tsp turmeric (optional, makes the "eggs" yellow)
½ tsp salt
⅛ tsp black pepper (optional)
Hot sauce to taste (optional)

1 Press Tofu: Place 6 paper towels on the counter. Drain tofu from package. Place block of tofu on the paper towels. Place a cutting board or baking sheet on top of tofu. Place 2 or 3 cans of beans or similar weight on top of the cutting board, and let sit for at least 15 minutes. This process gets excess water out of the tofu, allowing it space to soak in other incredible flavors.

2 Meanwhile, heat oil in a medium-sized skillet over medium-high heat. Reduce heat to medium-low and sauté veggies, spices, and salt until tender, about 5 minutes.

3 Crumble tofu into the skillet; continue to cook until heated through, about 5 minutes.

4 Serve warm topped with black pepper and hot sauce if desired.

5 Store leftovers in the fridge for up to 3 days.

Nutrition Snapshot
Per serving: 161 calories, 8.5 g total fat, 1 g saturated fat, 0 mg cholesterol, 298 mg sodium, 5 g carbohydrates, 2 g fiber, 1 g sugar, 15.5 g protein, 3% vitamin A, 54% vitamin C, 19.5% calcium, 13.5% iron

Makes 4 servings
Prep and cooking time 20 minutes

Confetti Pancakes

You may not know it, but pancakes are one of the best vegetable vehicles around. This sneaky recipe has shredded carrots and zucchini woven into the batter, and any other veggie can be substituted in the covert operation. Try cooked mashed cauliflower to keep the colors pancake-neutral. Add a few chocolate chips to each pancake and relish in your new title of Favorite Family Chef. Each tablespoon of pure maple syrup adds about 50 calories and 13 grams of sugar, so stretch your syrup by warming it in the microwave and spreading it more thinly over your plate.

2 cups whole wheat flour

4 tsp baking powder

½ tsp salt

1 Tbsp cinnamon

1 tsp sugar or agave nectar

2 cups (16 oz) vanilla almond milk, or other non-dairy milk

1 medium zucchini, shredded

2 medium carrots, shredded

2 Tbsp grapeseed oil, divided

1 In a large bowl, mix dry ingredients.

2 Add milk, shredded veggies, and 1 Tbsp oil, and stir together.

3 Heat remaining 1 Tbsp oil in a large skillet or pancake griddle over medium-high heat.

4 Reduce heat to medium-low and add batter, ¼ cup at a time, leaving about an inch between pancakes. Cook until bubbles start to form, about 7 minutes.

5 Flip pancakes and cook another 7 minutes.

6 Top with pure maple syrup, Organic Maple Agave Syrup Blend, or powdered sugar.

7 Store leftovers in the fridge for up to 3 days or in the freezer for up to 2 months. Pop them in the toaster for a quick breakfast anytime.

Nutrition Snapshot
Per pancake: 78 calories, 2 g total fat, 0 g saturated fat, 0 mg cholesterol, 194 mg sodium, 12.5 g carbohydrates, 2 g fiber, 2.5 g sugar, 2 g protein, 19.5% vitamin A, 1.5% vitamin C, 8.5% calcium, 4% iron

Note Once skillet is hot, pancakes will cook more quickly, about 5 minutes on each side.

Makes 18 4-inch round pancakes
Batter prep time 10 minutes
Cooking time 15 minutes per skillet batch

Mexican Potato Hash

Thanks to Gloria Huerta, a cooking instructor in North Hollywood, California who inspired this recipe, I now enjoy this spicy spin on hash browns several times a week. Accompany with fresh fruit, and serve with Eggless Eggs *(page 62) for a full-on brunch. This flexi dish can double as a hearty main dish served alongside an equally fierce veggie, such as the* Crave-Worthy Brussels Sprouts *(page 124). Rich in protein and fiber, this dish provides more than 100% the recommended intake of vitamin A.*

1 tsp grapeseed oil

2 large golden potatoes, scrubbed and cut into small chunks (preferably organic)

2 medium carrots, unpeeled, shredded or diced

½ cup filtered water

1 (12-oz) pkg Soy Chorizo, or 12 oz other meatless chorizo or sausages, diced

¼ cup chopped fresh cilantro (optional)

1 Heat oil in a large skillet over medium-high heat. Add potatoes and carrots and cook, covered, until potatoes start to brown, about 3 minutes.

2 Add water and chorizo; continue to cook, covered, stirring occasionally, until potatoes are tender, about 12 minutes.

3 Serve hot topped with fresh cilantro if desired.

4 Store leftovers in the fridge for up to 4 days.

Nutrition Snapshot
Per serving: 242 calories, 13.5 g total fat, 2 g saturated fat, 0 mg cholesterol, 871 mg sodium, 25.5 g carbohydrates, 7.5 g fiber, 5.5 g sugar, 13 g protein, 128% vitamin A, 30.5% vitamin C, 9.5% calcium, 21.5% iron

G Gluten Free

Makes 4 servings
Prep time 20 minutes

Pre-Game Show

I  Hummus

Is 2 tablespoons really 1 serving of hummus? Absolutely not, hummus lovers! But, considering how high-fat commercially prepared hummus can be, having a realistic ¼ or ½-cup serving could inch your fat intake up too high. This version is light on the tahini and olive oil and has its calories diffused with low-fat, high-fiber artichokes. Enjoy the liberal ½-cup serving with raw veggies, crackers, or right off the spoon.

1 (15-oz) can garbanzo beans, drained with liquid reserved
1 (14-oz) can artichoke hearts, drained
1 Tbsp tahini (sesame seed butter), or 2 Tbsp olive oil
¼ cup fresh-squeezed lemon juice
3 cloves garlic, or 3 cubes frozen Crushed Garlic
½ cup chopped fresh parsley (optional)
1 tsp cumin
¼ tsp black pepper

1 Combine ingredients in a blender or food processor and process until smooth. Add 2-3 tablespoons of reserved bean liquid for a thinner consistency. Dip and go!

2 Store leftovers in the fridge for up to 6 days.

Nutrition Snapshot
Per ½-cup serving: 110 calories, 2 g total fat, 0 g saturated fat, 0 mg cholesterol, 338 mg sodium, 18 g carbohydrates, 5.5 g fiber, 1 g sugar, 6.5 g protein, 10.5% vitamin A, 20% vitamin C, 6.5% calcium, 13% iron

Makes 6 (½-cup) servings
Prep time 5 minutes

Creamy Spinach Artichoke Dip

My dear friend, Elizabeth Korns of Washington D.C., inspired this dip as she yearned for a way to enjoy her mayo and Parmesan cheese stand-by without the post-dip remorse. Voilà! Indulge in this tasty creation with sliced veggies, crusty bread, or my personal favorite—Sesame Melba Round Crackers—at only 95 calories and 5 grams of fat per half-cup serving. The hot mayo and cheese version packs 300 calories and 30 grams total fat per half-cup serving. It's no contest!

1 (16-oz) bag frozen chopped spinach, thawed, and liquid drained (preferably organic)

1 (14-oz) can artichoke hearts, drained and chopped

1 (8-oz) container Tofutti Better Than Cream Cheese, or other non-dairy cream cheese

1 Tbsp lemon juice

1 tsp garlic powder

⅛ tsp salt

½ tsp dried dill weed (optional)

1 Thaw spinach in medium-sized microwave-safe bowl if necessary, and then squeeze and drain excess liquid. Add remaining ingredients to the bowl and stir together.

2 Serve cold, or hot by pouring the dip into a casserole dish and heating in a preheated 350° F oven, uncovered, for 20 minutes.

3 Store leftovers in the fridge for up to 4 days.

Nutrition Snapshot
Per ½-cup serving: 95 calories, 5 g total fat, 4 g saturated fat, 0 mg cholesterol, 286 mg sodium, 7.5 g carbohydrates, 2.5 g fiber, 1.5 g sugar, 3.5 g protein, 84% vitamin A, 11.5% vitamin C, 6% calcium, 4.5% iron

Makes 8 (½-cup) servings
Prep time 5 minutes for cold dip, 25 minutes for hot dip

No Fat Pants Nachos

A serving of traditional nachos has approximately 800 calories, 20 grams of fat, and will have you resorting to your fat pants in no time. Enjoy this version overloaded with veggies, beans, and hot sauce, and keep your fat pants in the closet. Eat these nachos as a snack or a well-rounded gluten-free meal.

2 oz Super Seeded Tortilla Chips (about 28 chips), or other multigrain tortilla chips

1 cup Refried Black Beans with Jalapeño Peppers (about ½ of the 16-oz can)

¼ cup filtered water

1 tomato, diced

½ green bell pepper, diced (preferably organic)

½ ripe avocado, cut into chunks

½ cup Chunky Salsa, or other favorite salsa

2 Tbsp chopped fresh cilantro (optional)

1 green onion, chopped

⅛ tsp salt

Hot sauce to taste (optional)

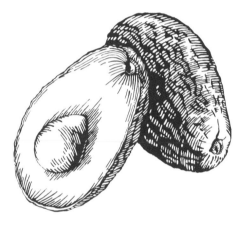

1 Layer chips on a large plate.

2 Heat the beans with water in a microwave-safe bowl or glass liquid measuring cup for 1-2 minutes. Pour evenly over chips.

3 Evenly distribute remaining ingredients. Chow down!

4 Leftover nachos will get soggy. Have a second serving.

Nutrition Snapshot
Per serving: 250 calories, 10.5 g total fat, 1 g saturated fat, 0 mg cholesterol, 671 mg sodium, 34.5 g carbohydrates, 8.5 g fiber, 4 g sugar, 8 g protein, 11.5% vitamin A, 53.5% vitamin C, 6.5% calcium, 18.5% iron

Ensure alternate multigrain chips are gluten-free

Makes 1 plate (3 servings)
Prep time 10 minutes

Fiery Cashew Dip

This recipe comes from Sandi Rechenmacher, a nutritional consultant and holistic health practitioner in Soquel, California. Enjoy the dip with rice crackers, flash-steamed veggies, or thinned with water as a topping for cooked vegetables.

1 cup roasted, unsalted cashew pieces

2 Tbsp sesame seeds

½ tsp garlic powder

½ cup of 14.5-oz can Diced and Fire Roasted Organic Tomatoes with Green Chiles, or other fire roasted tomatoes

2 Tbsp lemon juice

1 tsp reduced-sodium soy sauce

1 In a blender or food processor, process cashews, sesame seeds, and garlic powder.

2 Add remaining ingredients and process until smooth.

3 If you don't eat the entire recipe in one sitting, store leftovers in the fridge for up to 4 days.

Nutrition Snapshot
Per ¼-cup serving: 205 calories, 16.5 g total fat, 3.5 g saturated fat, 0 mg cholesterol, 122.5 mg sodium, 11 g carbohydrates, 2 g fiber, 3 g sugar, 6 g protein, 2.5% vitamin A, 10.5% vitamin C, 7% calcium, 10% iron

 Use tamari instead of soy sauce

Makes 4 (¼-cup) servings
Prep time 8 minutes

Polenta Stuffed Mini Peppers

These little beauties are not only a dinner party hit, but a perfect finger food for kids and kids-at-heart. Four pepper-halves supply nearly double the daily recommended intake of vitamin C. Enjoy them as an appetizer or side dish, and you may not be able to stop!

1 ½ dry pints (1 ½ pkg) Sweet Mini Peppers, about 14 mini peppers, cut in half lengthwise, stems and seeds removed

1 (18-oz) tube pre-cooked polenta

2 cups frozen chopped spinach, thawed (preferably organic)

1 Tbsp olive oil

1 tsp dried basil

1 tsp dried oregano

1 ½ tsp salt

1 Tbsp water

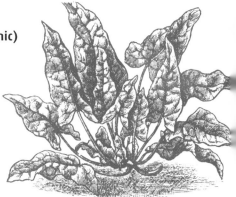

1 Preheat oven to 350° F.

2 In a medium-sized mixing bowl, mash polenta with a fork until light and fluffy.

3 Add spinach, oil, herbs, salt, and water, and stir together.

4 Place mini pepper halves open side up, side by side in a 9 x 13-inch baking dish.

5 Using your hands, form polenta mixture into 2-inch round balls and stuff each pepper half so that there's a mound on top of each pepper half.

6 Bake, uncovered, for 25 minutes, or until pepper halves are soft. Serve immediately.

7 Leftovers can be stored in the fridge for up to 3 days. Eat them cold or heat them up.

Nutrition Snapshot
Per 4 pepper-halves: 89 calories, 2 g total fat, 0.5 g saturated fat, 0 mg cholesterol, 751 mg sodium, 14.5 g carbohydrates, 2 g fiber, 3 g sugar, 2.5 g protein, 59% vitamin A, 190% vitamin C, 1.5% calcium, 3.5% iron

Tip Use just 1 package of mini peppers (about 10) and enjoy the remaining polenta stuffing as a side dish.

Note Use the same polenta filling to stuff mushrooms. Bake for 15 minutes at 350° F.

Makes 28 mini pepper halves (about 7 servings)
Prep time 15 minutes **Hands-off cooking time** 25 minutes

Grapeseed-Oil-Infused Tomato Spread

Christine Sproat—a great friend, busy mom, and pediatric occupational therapist—created this recipe after enjoying something similar at a posh restaurant. She realized she could be fancy right in the comfort of her own kitchen for a tenth of the cost and without having to hire a babysitter. Enjoy the spread with toasted slices of Olive Baguette and a good merlot.

1 (16-oz) pkg Mini Pearl Grape Tomatoes, or other grape tomatoes
6 cloves garlic, peeled
1 tsp sea salt
1 Tbsp grapeseed oil

1   Preheat oven to 400° F.

2   In a 9 x 9-inch baking dish, place tomatoes and garlic. Sprinkle with sea salt and drizzle oil over top.

3   Bake for 45 minutes, or until tomatoes start to brown.

4   Mash with potato masher or fork to break through garlic cloves and any remaining whole tomatoes. Stir mixture to combine.

5   Serve warm on crackers or baguette slices, or chill for 2 hours for a cold spread.

6   Store leftovers in the fridge for up to 5 days.

Nutrition Snapshot
Per ¼-cup serving: 56 calories, 2.5 g total fat, 0.5 g saturated fat, 0 mg cholesterol, 465.5 mg sodium, 7.5 g carbohydrates, <0.5 g fiber, 3 g sugar, 0 g protein, 8.5% vitamin A, 44.5% vitamin C, 0.5% calcium, 2.5% iron

Gluten Free
Serve on toasted gluten-free bread or rice crackers, such as Savory Thins

Makes 5 (¼-cup) servings
Prep time 3 minutes
Hands-off cooking time 45 minutes

Guacamame

Need nutrient justification for eating guacamole as a main dish? Voilà! By adding protein-rich edamame (green soy beans) to guac, you'll get a nifty balance of all the nutrients you need for a meal. Of course you can still enjoy this one as a snack, and a lower fat snack at that. High-fiber edamame drop the fat content by 8 grams and 65 calories per half-cup. Enjoy an extra scoop!

2 ripe avocados, peeled and pit removed
1 cup shelled edamame (green soy beans), thawed if frozen
½ onion, diced (purple adds yet another groovy color)
1 tomato, diced
Juice of 1 very ripe lemon
½ tsp sea salt

1 Using a potato masher, mash avocados with edamame beans, leaving some whole beans. If a less "beany" guacamole is desired, use a food processor or blender to process the avocados and beans until smooth.

2 Stir in remaining ingredients. Scoop with tortilla chips, just like you're used to.

3 Leftovers will last in the fridge for up to 2 days. To limit the browning effect of the avocados, toss the avocado pits in with the bowl of leftovers.

Nutrition Snapshot
Per ½-cup Serving: 175 calories, 12.5 g total fat, 1.5 g saturated fat, 0 mg cholesterol, 244.5 mg sodium, 12.5 g carbohydrates, 7 g fiber, 0.5 g sugar, 7 g protein, 5% vitamin A, 23% vitamin C, 4% calcium, 6.5% iron

Gluten Free

Makes 5 (½-cup) servings
Prep Time 5 minutes

Tofurella Sticks

This scrumptious spin on mozzarella sticks is low in saturated fat, cholesterol-free, and a high-protein snack. Kids love to dip them, and parents love to watch their kids eating tofu!

1 (15-oz) block of extra firm tofu
½ cup panko breadcrumbs, or other breadcrumbs
1 tsp dried basil
1 tsp dried oregano
½ tsp salt
3 Tbsp grapeseed oil, divided
½ cup Tomato Basil Marinara Sauce, or other marinara

1 Press Tofu: Place 6 paper towels on the counter. Drain tofu from package. Place block of tofu on the paper towels. Place a cutting board or baking sheet (something totally flat) on top of tofu. Place a can of beans or similar weight on top of the cutting board, and let sit for at least 30 minutes. This process gets excess water out of the tofu, allowing it space to soak in other incredible flavors, and giving it a firmer texture. For these sticks, the longer you can press the tofu, the better the final texture will be. But, even just pressing it for 30 minutes until the paper towels are soaked, will help immensely.

2 Cut tofu into 12 strips.

3 In a small bowl, combine breadcrumbs, basil, oregano, and salt.

4 In a separate small bowl, pour 2 Tbsp oil.

5 In a medium-sized skillet over medium-high heat, heat remaining 1 Tbsp oil.

6 Dip each tofu slice in bowl of oil and then roll in breadcrumb mixture. Place tofu in the skillet and cook over medium-high heat flipping until browned, about 3 minutes on each side.

7 Serve dipped in marinara.

8 Store leftovers in the fridge for up to 3 days.

Nutrition Snapshot

Per stick: 86 calories, 6 g total fat, 0.5 g saturated fat, 0 mg cholesterol, 150 mg sodium, 2.5 g carbohydrates, <0.5 g fiber, 0.5 g sugar, 5.5 g protein, 2% vitamin A, 1% vitamin C, 6.5% calcium, 4.5% iron

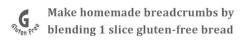

Make homemade breadcrumbs by blending 1 slice gluten-free bread

Makes 12 sticks
Prep time 25 minutes once tofu is pressed
Hands-off prep time 30 minutes for pressing the tofu

Black Bean Dip

With enormous flavor, zero grams of fat, over 5 grams of fiber, and nearly half the daily requirement of iron per half-cup serving, this dip is a crowd pleaser no matter what the occasion. Enjoy it with tortilla chips, raw vegetables, or as a tortilla or sandwich spread.

1 (15-oz) can black beans, drained and rinsed
1 cup salsa
½ tsp ground cumin (optional)

1 Combine all ingredients in a food processor or blender and process until smooth, scraping down sides with a rubber spatula as needed.

2 Eat cool or heated up in the microwave for a minute.

3 Store leftovers in the fridge for up to 5 days.

Nutrition Snapshot
Per ½-cup serving: 116 calories, 0 g total fat, 0 g saturated fat, 0 mg cholesterol, 268 mg sodium, 20.5 g carbohydrates, 5.5 g fiber, 6 g sugar, 5.5 g protein, 4% vitamin A, 7.5% vitamin C, 6% calcium, 43.5% iron

G
Gluten Free

Makes 4 (½-cup) servings
Prep time 5 minutes

Lentil Pâté

Spread this tangy pâté on Sesame Melba Rounds, toasted baguette slices, or pipe it into hollowed-out cherry tomatoes or steamed and hollowed-out Brussels sprouts. It even works well as a sandwich spread. Heck, eat it right off the spoon for breakfast. You only live once!

1 (17.6-oz) pkg refrigerated Steamed Lentils, or 2 ½ cups cooked lentils

5 cloves garlic, peeled

12 large pitted black olives

3 Tbsp capers, with juice

2 Tbsp lemon juice

1 Tbsp olive oil

1 Tbsp chopped fresh rosemary (optional)

¼ tsp salt

⅛ tsp black pepper

1 In a food processor or powerful blender, process all ingredients together until combination is a smooth paste (some chunks may remain).

2 Store leftovers in the fridge for up to 5 days.

Nutrition Snapshot
Per ¼-cup serving: 82 calories, 2 g total fat, 0.5 g saturated fat, 0 mg cholesterol, 302 mg sodium, 11 g carbohydrates, 4.5 g fiber, 1 g sugar, 4.5 g protein, 0.5% vitamin A, 3.5% vitamin C, 2% calcium, 11.5% iron

Makes 10 (¼-cup) servings
Prep time 10 minutes

Soups & Stews

17 Bean Soup for a Crowd

Is dried bean soup mix one of those things you zoom past in the store for fear that it might jump into your cart? Fear no more! Trader Joe's 17 Bean & Barley Mix, or any 1-pound bag of dried bean soup mix is a simple, scrumptious way to feed a whole flock for just a few dollars. This recipe "beefs up" the beans with colorful tomatoes, spinach, carrots, Soy Chorizo, and a spice combo that brings it all home. Enjoy a cup of this soup with multigrain bread or crackers, and a side salad such as the Blink-of-An-Eye Green Salad *(page 108).*

1 (16-oz) pkg 17 Bean & Barley Mix, or other 1-lb dried bean soup mix

4 cups filtered water

1 (28-oz) can diced tomatoes

1 (6-oz) bag prewashed raw baby spinach (preferably organic)

1 onion, diced

3 carrots, finely chopped

1 (12-oz) pkg Soy Chorizo, or about 12 oz other meatless chorizo or sausages, chopped

2 Tbsp 21 Seasoning Salute, or other sodium-free spice mix

2 tsp salt

Hot sauce to taste (optional)

1 Quick soak for bean mix: In a large soup pot, combine soup mix with about 6 cups filtered water and 1 tsp baking soda (optional for making beans less gassy). Bring to a boil, then reduce heat to medium and cook uncovered for 2-3 minutes. Remove from heat and soak for 1 hour. Drain.

2 Add 4 cups filtered water and remaining ingredients to beans (which have been soaked and drained) and bring to a boil. Reduce heat to simmer, and cook for 1 hour. Add hot sauce if desired.

3 Store leftovers in the fridge for up to 4 days or in the freezer for up to 2 months.

Nutrition Snapshot

Per cup: 226 calories, 3.5 g total fat, 0 g saturated fat, 0 mg cholesterol, 591 mg sodium, 37 g carbohydrates, 12 g fiber, 4.5 g sugar, 13.5 g protein, 58.5% vitamin A, 18% vitamin C, 8.5% calcium, 23% iron

Slow-Cooker Option: Do "quick soak" or soak beans overnight with 6 cups filtered water plus baking soda. Drain water in the morning. Add remaining ingredients and slow-cook on low heat for 6 hours.

Makes 17 (1-cup) servings
Prep time 20 minutes
Hands-off cooking time 2 hours
Slow-cooker 6-7 hours

Carrot Ginger Soup

The bold touch of ginger in this soup gives it real personality. Ginger is especially helpful in easing digestion, which helps to relieve nausea, an upset stomach, and even motion sickness. The high carrot content helps you get nearly 300% of the daily requirement of vitamin A. All that for under 150 calories a serving! Health never tasted so good.

1 Tbsp olive oil

4 cloves garlic, chopped

1 small yellow onion, chopped

1 large chunk of ginger, about the size of a golf ball, peeled and chopped

4 cups water or vegetable stock

½ tsp 21 Seasoning Salute or other salt-free spice blend (omit if using vegetable stock instead of water)

½ tsp salt (omit if using vegetable stock instead of water)

2 lbs carrots, washed, unpeeled, and cut into large chunks

1 (15-oz) can garbanzo beans or white kidney beans, drained

1 Tbsp agave nectar or pure maple syrup

1 Tbsp Earth Balance Natural Buttery Spread, or other non-hydrogenated margarine

1 In a large soup pot over medium-high heat, heat olive oil and sauté garlic, onion, and ginger for 5 minutes until onion becomes translucent.

2 Add remaining ingredients and bring to a boil until carrots are soft. Blend soup in batches until entire pot is blended, and return it to the soup pot. Serve immediately, or reheat when you're ready to enjoy it.

3 Store leftovers in the fridge for up to 5 days, or in the freezer for up to 2 months.

Nutrition Snapshot

Per cup: 141 calories, 3.5 g total fat, 0.5 g saturated fat, 0 mg cholesterol, 270 mg sodium, 23.5 g carbohydrates, 7.5 g fiber, 8 g sugar, 5 g protein, 273% vitamin A, 12% vitamin C, 8.5% calcium, 6.5% iron

Tip To peel ginger, use the edge of a small metal spoon rather than a peeler. The skin will come off easily around all the bumps and lumps.

Tip Don't waste time finely dicing the garlic, onions, and ginger since you'll be blending them later. Just chop them enough for the sautéing to bring out their wonderful flavors.

Safety Tip While blending hot soup, don't fill the blender jar more than half full. Cover the lid with a dry towel, and hold it down with your hand while blending so the steam doesn't shoot the lid (and soup) up to your kitchen ceiling. Depending on how powerful your blender is, you may need to use some force to keep the lid on.

G
Gluten Free

Makes 8 (1-cup) servings
Prep and cooking time 30 minutes

Gazpacho à la Shepherd Street

Puerto Rican native and family friend Rafael Prieto started making and perfecting Gazpacho when he couldn't keep up with his tomato and cucumber crops on Shepherd Street in Northwest Washington, D.C. This no-longer-secret recipe creates a refreshing soup that can be served cold or hot, chunky or soupy, from a glass or a bowl, and often topped with croutons. You really can't do it wrong!

4 ripe tomatoes

1 large cucumber, peeled if not organic

¼ red onion

½ red bell pepper (preferably organic)

½ green bell pepper (preferably organic)

4 cloves garlic

2 Tbsp olive oil

3 Tbsp red wine vinegar

¼ tsp black pepper

½ tsp salt

Hot sauce to taste (optional)

Croutons or avocado chunks for garnish (optional)

1 Blend all ingredients (except for hot sauce and croutons) until smooth or desired consistency. Serve immediately (because you can't wait), or chill in the fridge for at least 1 hour to let flavors marry.

2 Top individual servings with hot sauce, a few croutons, and/or a couple avocado chunks if desired.

Nutrition Snapshot
Per cup: 89 calories, 5.5 g total fat, 0.5 g saturated fat, 0 mg cholesterol, 243 mg sodium, 9.5 g carbohydrates, 2.5 g fiber, 1.5 g sugar, 1.5 g protein, 26.5% vitamin A, 58.5% vitamin C, 2% calcium, 4% iron

G Gluten Free **Omit croutons**

Makes 5 (1-cup) servings
Prep time 10 minutes

Curried Lentil Stew

Like peanut butter and chocolate, lentils and curry are a beautiful marriage. Enjoy this stew as a hearty appetizer, side dish, or main course with crusty bread. If you're feeling extra daring, put in the full bag of Southern Greens Blend—a healthy recommendation by my father-in-law and greens enthusiast Michael Reilly.

1 Tbsp olive oil

1 small onion, diced

2 cloves garlic, minced, or 2 cubes frozen Crushed Garlic

2 Tbsp curry powder

3 cups filtered water

2 tomatoes, chopped

3 carrots, diced

3 celery stalks, sliced (preferably organic)

½ (16-oz) bag Southern Greens Blend, or 1 bunch kale, collards, or other dark leafy green, ripped into pieces

2 (17.6-oz) pkgs refrigerated Steamed Lentils, or 5 cups cooked lentils

1 tsp salt

1 In a large soup pot over medium-high heat, sauté onion, garlic, and curry powder in olive oil until onion is translucent, about 4 minutes.

2 Add remaining ingredients and bring to a boil. Reduce heat to simmer and cook, covered, 10 minutes. Serve piping hot.

3 Store leftovers in the fridge for up to 5 days or in the freezer for up to 2 months.

Nutrition Snapshot
Per cup: 145 calories, 1.5 g total fat, 0 g saturated fat, 0 mg cholesterol, 459 mg sodium, 23.5 g carbohydrates, 9 g fiber, 2.5 g sugar, 9.5 g protein, 54.5% vitamin A, 17% vitamin C, 6.5% calcium, 23% iron

Gluten Free

Makes 11 (1-cup) servings
Prep and cooking time 20 minutes

Broccoli Leek Soup

Blended soup is a great way to get kids (and adults) to eat more broccoli. If green foods don't generally go over well among the group, use cauliflower instead of broccoli and this soup will be just as nutritious. The whole cruciferous family of vegetables (including broccoli, cauliflower, kale, collards, Brussels sprouts, cabbage, and rutabaga) are incredible sources of vitamin C, fiber, and potent anti-cancer compounds. Among their many qualities, these powerhouses speed up the removal of estrogen from the body therefore decreasing breast cancer risk and increasing survival.

3 cups filtered water

2 large golden potatoes, unpeeled, scrubbed, and cut into chunks

1 (16-oz) bag frozen Sliced Leeks, or 2 large fresh leeks, ends removed and sliced

2 stalks broccoli, florets broken into pieces and stalk chopped

4 cloves garlic, peeled and left whole, or 4 cubes frozen Crushed Garlic

2 Tbsp Earth Balance Natural Buttery Spread, or other non-hydrogenated margarine

1 ½ tsp salt

¼ tsp black pepper

Hot sauce to taste (optional)

1 In a large soup pot over high heat, combine water and remaining ingredients as they're prepared. Bring to a boil and cook, covered, until potatoes are soft, about 5 minutes.

2 Transfer in batches to a blender and blend until smooth, placing blended portions in a large bowl until all soup is blended.

3 Return blended soup to the soup pot. Serve immediately, or reheat when you're ready to enjoy it.

4 Top with hot sauce if desired.

5 Store leftovers in the fridge for up to 4 days or in the freezer for up to 2 months.

Nutrition Snapshot
Per cup: 86 calories, 2.5 g total fat, 1 g saturated fat, 0 mg cholesterol, 435 mg sodium, 14.5 g carbohydrates, 2.5 g fiber, 3 g sugar, 2.5 g protein, 18.5% vitamin A, 68.5% vitamin C, 4.5% calcium, 7.5% iron

Safety Tip See *Carrot Ginger Soup*, page 95

Makes 9 (1-cup) servings
Prep and cooking time 20 minutes

G
Gluten Free

Keller's Basil Stew

This recipe was invented by my daughter Keller at age 4, and has become a household staple. Keller would eat basil at every meal if she had her way, and often requests bags of it in her lunch box. She recommends a hearty hunk of Olive Baguette to accompany the stew. However, if brownies came her way, those would work too.

1 tsp olive oil

½ yellow onion, diced

2 medium carrots, unpeeled, diced

½ tsp garlic powder

½ tsp salt

1 (28-oz) can Tuscano Marinara Sauce, or other marinara sauce

2 tomatoes, diced

1 (10-oz) pkg sliced white mushrooms

1 (2.5-oz) pkg fresh basil, leaves pulled from stems and torn in half (about 40 medium-sized leaves)

1 (15-oz) can garbanzo beans, drained

1 cup filtered water

1   In a large soup pot over medium-high heat, sauté onion, carrots, garlic, and salt in olive oil until onion is translucent, about 5 minutes.

2   Add remaining ingredients and bring to a boil. Reduce heat to simmer and cook, covered, until mushrooms are tender, about 5 minutes.

3   Store leftovers in the fridge for up to 5 days or in the freezer for up to 2 months.

Nutrition Snapshot
Per cup: 142 calories, 2.5 g total fat, 0 g saturated fat, 0 mg cholesterol, 585 mg sodium, 22 g carbohydrates, 8.5 g fiber, 6 g sugar, 6 g protein, 50.5% vitamin A, 10.5% vitamin C, 2% calcium, 8% iron

G Gluten Free

Makes 8 (1-cup) servings
Prep and cooking time 20 minutes

Curried Sweet Potato Soup

Sweet potatoes are that much tastier with a little zip and zing. This simple fat-free soup is overloaded with vision-enhancing and immune-boosting beta-carotene, the water-soluble form of vitamin A. Each cup of soup has nearly a days-worth of vitamin A. Enjoy it with a green salad and multigrain crackers.

5 small sweet potatoes, unpeeled, scrubbed, and cut into chunks

5 cups filtered water

1 small onion, chopped

3 cloves garlic

2 tsp curry powder

½ tsp salt

¼ cup chopped cilantro for garnish (optional)

1 In a large soup pot over high heat, bring all ingredients except cilantro to a boil. Reduce heat to medium-high and cook until sweet potatoes are tender, about 8 minutes.

2 Transfer in batches to a blender and blend until smooth, placing blended portions in a large bowl until all soup is blended.

3 Return blended soup to pot and serve immediately, or cook further if needed.

4 Top each serving with cilantro if desired.

5 Store leftovers in the fridge for up to 4 days or in the freezer for up to 2 months.

Nutrition Snapshot
Per cup: 64 calories, 0 g total fat, 0 g saturated fat, 0 mg cholesterol, 169 mg sodium, 14.5 g carbohydrates, 2.5 g fiber, 5.5 g sugar, 1.5 g protein, 77% vitamin A, 17% vitamin C, 2.5% calcium, 5% iron

Tip Peeling sweet potatoes is labor-intensive and strips them of valuable fiber and nutrients. Scrub them, leave the peels on, and eat them that much sooner!

Safety Tip See *Carrot Ginger Soup*, page 95

Serve with rice crackers, such as Savory Thins

Makes 8 (1-cup) servings
Prep and cooking time 20 minutes

Cool Veggies

Blink-of-An-Eye Green Salad

Gone are the days when eating a salad meant laboring for hours over a sink and cutting board. You can make this one as you're walking to the dinner table!

1 (7-oz) bag Butter Lettuce, or other prewashed bag of salad greens
2 Tbsp olive oil
2 tsp brown rice vinegar
¼ tsp sea salt

1 Place greens in a medium-sized bowl. Add remaining ingredients and toss.

2 Leftover salad will not keep, so get seconds!

Nutrition Snapshot
Per serving: 132 calories, 13.5 g total fat, 2 g saturated fat, 0 mg cholesterol, 290 mg sodium, 2.5 g carbohydrates, 1.5 g fiber, 1 g sugar, 1.5 g protein, 75% vitamin A, 7.5% vitamin C, 2.5% calcium, 8% iron

Note Sea salt has a great taste in salads and fresh foods, but any type of salt could be used.

G
Gluten Free

Makes 2 servings
Prep time 3 minutes

Arugula Salad with Pan-Seared Butternut Squash

Searing is a great way to bring out the flavors in veggies, and it's done by cooking them in a skillet with high heat and very little oil, a good way to keep the fat content down. Enjoy this colorful salad in the fall when squash is aplenty.

1 tsp olive oil

2 cups very small butternut squash cubes (about the top portion of a butternut squash, peeled and finely cubed)

¼ tsp salt

¼ tsp garlic powder

1 (7-oz) bag Wild Arugula Wild Rocket Salad, or other bag of prewashed arugula

2 Tbsp white balsamic vinegar, divided

Dash of sesame seeds for garnish (optional)

1 In a medium-sized skillet, heat oil. Add butternut squash chunks, salt, and garlic powder. Pan-sear the squash for 6 minutes stirring it every minute or so and removing it from the heat for 10 seconds at a time if the pan gets too smoky. Remove from heat and place on a plate in the fridge for 5 minutes to cool.

2 Divide bag of arugula onto 2 plates. Top each plate with the butternut squash cubes and 1 Tbsp of white balsamic vinegar. Garnish each one with sesame seeds if desired.

3 Dressed salad will not last past the current meal, so eat up! Butternut squash cubes make perfect finger foods for toddlers or toothpick veggie kebabs for young children.

Nutrition Snapshot
Per serving: 143 calories, 3 g total fat, 0.5 g saturated fat, 0 mg cholesterol, 325 mg sodium, 30 g carbohydrates, 7 g fiber, 6 g sugar, 4 g protein, 327% vitamin A, 71.5% vitamin C, 23.5% calcium, 13% iron

Gluten Free

Makes 2 servings
Prep and cooking time 15 minutes

Mango Summer Salad

This refreshing salad is based on a summertime invention by Jan Graves, a photographer by day and cooking instructor by night in Arlington, Virginia. She enjoys a supersized helping on hot summer days.

5 oz (½ bag) Sorrento Baby Arugula Blend, or other baby arugula

6 fresh basil leaves, chopped

1 ripe mango, peeled and cut into chunks*

1 cucumber, peeled if not organic, and cut into small chunks

1 medium tomato

1 ear of white corn, cut off the cob (uncooked), or 1 cup frozen Cut White Corn, thawed

1 (15-oz) can garbanzo beans, drained and rinsed

¼ cup white balsamic vinegar

2 Tbsp Raw Blanched Slivered Almonds

1 In a large salad bowl, toss all ingredients, and serve.

2 Because there isn't any oil in this recipe, leftovers will keep in an airtight container in the fridge for up to 2 days (oil wilts the lettuce immediately).

Nutrition Snapshot

Per serving (¼ of recipe): 206 calories, 3.5 g total fat, 0 g saturated fat, 0 mg cholesterol, 369 mg sodium, 39.5 g carbohydrates, 8 g fiber, 15.5 g sugar, 9 g protein, 56% vitamin A, 39.5% vitamin C, 5% calcium, 9% iron

* *Tip* The porcupine method for cutting a mango: Using a sharp knife, carefully slice all the way down alongside the seed on the narrower side of the mango. Repeat along the other side of the seed. Score cross-hatch lines in each fruit half, almost all the way to the skin, but without piercing it. Turn the skin inside-out to eat on its own, or slice off each chunk with a small paring knife. Slice remaining flesh off from around the seed.

Makes 4 servings or 2 meal-size servings
Prep time 20 minutes

Lenticchie all'Arancia (Lentils and Oranges)

This simple Italian lentil dish will have you saying "delizioso" in no time! Enjoy it with Simple Spaghetti Squash *(page 135) or over a bed of greens. Lentils are a stellar source of iron, fiber, and protein—that's a lot of power for a little dude!*

1 (17.6-oz) pkg refrigerated Steamed Lentils, rinsed, or 2 ½ cups cooked and chilled lentils

2 ripe navel oranges, peeled and cut into small pieces

½ purple onion, diced

5 stalks celery, diced (preferably organic)

¼ cup chopped fresh parsley

1 Tbsp olive oil

2 Tbsp Orange Muscat Champagne Vinegar

⅛ tsp sea salt

1 In a large salad bowl, stir together all ingredients. Serve immediately, or chill in the fridge for 30 minutes to let the flavors solidify their marriage.

2 Store leftovers in the fridge for up to 3 days.

Nutrition Snapshot
Per serving: 234 calories, 3.5 g total fat, 0.5 g saturated fat, 0 mg cholesterol, 418 mg sodium, 37 g carbohydrates, 12.5 g fiber, 4.5 g sugar, 12.5 g protein, 9% vitamin A, 75% vitamin C, 7.5% calcium, 27.5% iron

Makes 4 servings
Prep time 15 minutes

G
Gluten Free

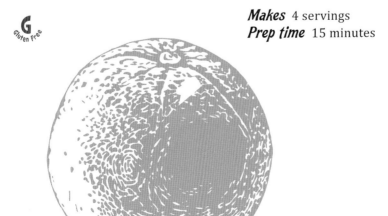

Kaleidoscope Bean Salad

Need a healthy potluck dish, but don't have a lot of time to prepare it? This colorful salad will wow the masses with only a few minutes of prep and a handful of ingredients. Feature it as a super side dish, blend it into a bean dip, stuff it into a burrito, toss it into soup, or serve atop a bed of greens.

½ **purple onion, diced**

1 **red bell pepper, diced (preferably organic)**

1 **(15-oz) can pinto beans, drained and rinsed**

1 **(15-oz) can kidney beans, drained and rinsed**

1 **cup shelled edamame (green soy beans), thawed if frozen**

1 **cup frozen corn kernels, thawed**

¼ **cup Light Champagne Vinaigrette, or other low-fat vinaigrette dressing**

⅛ **tsp sea salt**

1 In a large mixing bowl, stir together all ingredients.

2 Store leftovers in the fridge for up to 3 days.

Nutrition Snapshot
Per serving: 216 calories, 3.5 g total fat, 0.5 g saturated fat, 0 mg cholesterol, 390 mg sodium, 35.5 g carbohydrates, 11 g fiber, 4 g sugar, 13 g protein, 3% vitamin A, 44% vitamin C, 9.5% calcium, 14% iron

Makes 6 (1-cup) servings
Prep time 5 minutes

Garden Grower's Special

One summer, our cucumber and tomato plants produced way more than expected, and this recipe was born. Enjoy this refreshing salad with a hot baguette and a cool Chardonnay.

1 pint grape tomatoes, cut in half, or 2 large vine-ripened tomatoes, cut into chunks
2 medium cucumbers, peeled if not organic, cut into chunks
½ red onion, diced
3 Tbsp brown rice vinegar
½ tsp sea salt
¼ tsp black pepper

1 In a medium-sized salad bowl, combine all ingredients and toss. Serve immediately.

2 Store leftovers in the fridge for up to 2 days.

Nutrition Snapshot
Per serving: 101 calories, 0.5 g total fat, 0 g saturated fat, 0 mg cholesterol, 588 mg sodium, 22.5 g carbohydrates, 2.5 g fiber, 5 g sugar, 2.5 g protein, 26.5% vitamin A, 95% vitamin C, 4.5% calcium, 8.5% iron

G
Gluten Free

Makes 2 servings
Prep time 5 minutes

Tofu Feta, Walnut, and Beet Salad

Think warm goat cheese salad without the fat, without the goat, and with ALL the flavor. The dill and white balsamic add a beautiful touch to the flavor mélange. Enjoy this salad alongside a bowl of Carrot Ginger Soup (page 94) and warm multigrain bread.

2 tsp grapeseed oil

½ (15-oz) block organic firm tofu, drained and pressed for 10 minutes*

1 tsp salt

½ tsp dried dill weed

1 (6-oz) bag baby spinach (preferably organic)

1 (10-oz) bag shredded green cabbage

1 (8-oz) pkg Steamed & Peeled Baby Beets, drained and cut into strips, or 6 small beets, peeled, boiled, and cut into strips

¼ cup white balsamic vinegar

¼ cup whole walnuts

1 In a medium-sized skillet over high heat, heat oil, tofu, salt, and dill, crushing tofu into crumbles and stirring until tofu begins to brown, about 7 minutes.

2 On each of 4 plates, place ¼ of the spinach, followed by ¼ of the cabbage, ¼ of the beets, ¼ of the tofu mixture, 1 Tbsp balsamic, and 1 Tbsp walnuts. Serve immediately.

3 Leftovers don't keep well, but the tofu mixture and other ingredients can be stored in the fridge and kept on hand for up to 5 days for easy salad making.

Nutrition Snapshot
Per serving: 176 calories, 9.5 g total fat, 1 g saturated fat, 0 mg cholesterol, 650 mg sodium, 13.5 g carbohydrates, 4.5 g fiber, 8.5 g sugar, 9.5 g protein, 46% vitamin A, 59.5% vitamin C, 13.5% calcium, 18% iron

*See The Big Tofu (page 163) for how to press tofu.

G
Gluten Free

Makes 4 servings
Prep and cooking time 20 minutes

Crave-Worthy Brussels Sprouts

If you've only experimented with frozen Brussels sprouts, then this recipe is a must-try. Fresh Brussels sprouts have a delightful crunch and are loaded with filling fiber and immune-boosting vitamin C, and this recipe couldn't be easier in getting you to your goal. Enjoy a heaping helping of these with Hot Chickpea Burgers *(page 153).*

30 fresh Brussels sprouts, plucked, rinsed, and cut in half length-wise

1 Tbsp olive oil

2 Tbsp water

1 tsp garlic powder

½ tsp salt

⅛ tsp black pepper

½ tsp crushed red pepper (optional)

1 Heat oil in a large skillet over medium-high heat. Toss in the Brussels sprouts until they get frisky (the point at which you turn on your overhead fan). Add the water, cover, and cook 5-10 minutes.

2 Remove cover, sprinkle with garlic powder, salt, black pepper, and crushed red pepper if using; continue to cook until Brussels sprouts are toasty brown. Serve immediately.

3 Store leftovers in the fridge for up to 3 days.

Nutrition Snapshot
Per serving (12 Brussels sprout halves): 76 calories, 3 g total fat, 0.5 g saturated fat, 0 mg cholesterol, 261 mg sodium, 10.5 g carbohydrates, 4.5 g fiber, 2.5 g sugar, 4 g protein, 17% vitamin A, 161.5% vitamin C, 5% calcium, 9% iron

G Gluten Free

Makes 5 servings
Prep and cooking time 20 minutes

Roasted Reds

Red peppers are loaded with cancer-kicking and immune-boosting beta-carotene, and roasting brings out their sweet, rich flavor. Toss ½ cup of these roasted beauties into I ♥ Hummus (page 71), atop whole wheat pasta, or simply enjoy them as an appetizer or side dish. A generous 1-cup serving has nearly double the recommended daily intake of vitamin A (disguised as beta-carotene) and nearly 5 times the recommended daily intake of vitamin C.

5 red bell peppers, cut into bite-size pieces (preferably organic)
1 Tbsp olive oil
1 tsp garlic powder
½ cup chopped fresh basil
⅛ tsp salt

1 Preheat oven to 400° F.

2 Evenly distribute sliced red peppers into a 9 x 13-inch baking dish. Drizzle with oil, and sprinkle with garlic powder, basil, and salt. Bake for 60 minutes, stirring once halfway through.

3 Store leftovers in the fridge for up to 4 days.

Nutrition Snapshot
Per serving: 74 calories, 4 g total fat, 0.5 g saturated fat, 0 mg cholesterol, 108 mg sodium, 10 g carbohydrates, 3.5 g fiber, 0 g sugar, 2 g protein, 175% vitamin A, 473% vitamin C, 2% calcium, 5% iron

Makes 4 servings
Prep time 5 minutes
Hands–off cooking time 60 minutes

Garlicky Potatoes and Greens

Looking for a filling veggie side dish that only takes a few minutes of prep? Search no more! This combo can be prepped in just 10 minutes, and then tossed in the oven for an hour while you tend to your garden, put laundry away, or just chill with a refreshing brewski. Dark leafy greens are loaded with highly absorbable calcium, iron, and folate (from the word "foliage"). Plus, the greens, potatoes, and green pepper are all incredible sources of immune-boosting vitamin C, which even helps increase iron absorption. One serving of this recipe gives you more than a full day's requirement for vitamin C. Take that, citrus!

1 (16-oz) bag Southern Greens Blend, or 2 bunches mustard greens, turnip greens, collards or kale, stems removed and torn into 2-inch square–shape pieces

3 golden or large red potatoes, scrubbed, unpeeled, and cut into chunks (preferably organic)

1 green bell pepper, cut into bite-size pieces (preferably organic)

2 tsp garlic powder

½ tsp salt

2 Tbsp olive oil

1 Preheat oven to 375° F.

2 In a 9 x 13-inch baking dish, combine all the veggies, sprinkle them with garlic powder and salt, and drizzle with oil. Carefully stir veggies to coat evenly. The mountain of veggies will cook down to about half its size.

3 Bake for 1 hour, stirring after 30 minutes, and then again after 1 hour. Serve hot.

4 Store leftovers in the fridge for up to 4 days.

Nutrition Snapshot
Per serving: 203 calories, 7 g total fat, 1 g saturated fat, 0 mg cholesterol, 327 mg sodium, 31.5 g carbohydrates, 5 g fiber, 1 g sugar, 5.5 g protein, 62% vitamin A, 107% vitamin C, 16% calcium, 39% folate, 13.5% iron

Makes 3 servings
Prep time 10 minutes
Hands-off cooking time 60 minutes

Thai Basil Eggplant, Yowza! (Pud Makua Yow)

This popular Thai dish is a quick way to go through some overgrowing garden basil, but also a simple and scrumptious way to enjoy eggplant. Serve it with The Big Tofu *(page 163) over* Perfect Brown Rice *(page 234).*

1 Tbsp grapeseed or vegetable oil

2-3 red chili peppers, finely chopped, or 1-2 tsp crushed red pepper flakes

4 cloves garlic, finely chopped

2 large eggplants, cut into chunks

1 cup filtered water

1 Tbsp sugar

3 Tbsp reduced-sodium soy sauce

1 bunch fresh basil, stems removed (about 1-2 cups leaves)

1 In a large skillet over medium-high heat, sauté peppers and garlic in oil until the garlic is golden brown. Add eggplant and water, stir, cover, and cook 7-10 minutes until eggplant is cooked.

2 Add sugar and soy sauce, stir, and cook another 2 minutes. Remove from heat.

3 Just before serving, stir in basil.

4 Store leftovers in the fridge for up to 3 days.

Nutrition Snapshot
Per serving: 140 calories, 4 g total fat, 0.5 g saturated fat, 0 mg cholesterol, 355 mg sodium, 24.5 g carbohydrates, 7.5 g fiber, 5 g sugar, 3.5 g protein, 15% vitamin A, 102% vitamin C, 3.5% calcium, 7% iron

G Gluten Free
Use tamari instead of soy sauce

Makes 4 servings
Prep and cooking time 20 minutes

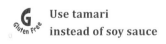

Sesame Greens

Dark leafy greens like mustard greens, turnip greens, and collards are incredible sources of calcium with double the absorption of dairy calcium. Given the Popeye powers associated with eating dark greens, this recipe couldn't be an easier or tastier way to energize you. Need an extra kick? Enjoy a double serving for just 175 calories!

½ cup filtered water

2 tsp toasted sesame oil

5 oz (½ bag) Shredded Carrots, or 2 medium carrots, shredded or cut into thin strips

1 red bell pepper, cut into thin strips (preferably organic)

1 (16-oz) bag Southern Greens Blend, or 1 bunch kale, collards, or other dark leafy green, ripped into pieces

1 Tbsp brown rice vinegar

2 tsp sesame seeds

3 Tbsp reduced-sodium soy sauce

1 In a large pot, steam carrots and red bell pepper in water and sesame oil over medium-high heat, about 2 minutes. Add greens, rice vinegar, and sesame seeds, cover and steam for another 5 minutes until greens are tender. Remove from heat.

2 Mix using a pasta grabber or tongs. Add soy sauce just prior to serving—it will turn the greens from bright to blah if it sits on them too long. Serve with pasta grabber or tongs so any remaining cooking liquid remains in the pot.

3 Store leftovers in the fridge for up to 3 days.

Nutrition Snapshot
Per serving: 88 calories, 3 g total fat, 0.5 g saturated fat, 0 mg cholesterol, 403 mg sodium, 11 g carbohydrates, 4.5 g fiber, 4 g sugar, 4 g protein, 113% vitamin A, 99% vitamin C, 18% calcium, 13% iron

Alternate option: Reserve the sesame seeds and top each serving with ½ tsp.

 Use tamari instead of soy sauce

Makes 4 servings
Prep and cooking time 10 minutes

Simple Spaghetti Squash

This addictively simple dish was adapted from a recipe by Janet McKee, a Holistic Health Counselor in Pittsburgh, Pennsylvania. Toss the squash into the oven first thing in the morning while you get ready for the day, and you'll have it ready for lunch or dinner. The post-bake prep is as easy as opening a jar of marinara sauce. Now that's a veggie side dish even busy folks can manage!

1 spaghetti squash, carefully cut in half and then half again, seeds scooped out

½ tsp salt

2 cups Organic Tomato Basil Marinara Sauce, or other marinara sauce

Hot sauce to taste (optional)

12 fresh basil leaves for garnish (optional)

1 Preheat oven to 400° F.

2 Place the cut sides of spaghetti squash down in a baking dish or roasting pan with about 1 inch of water. Roast for 1 hour or until soft.

3 Once the squash is finished cooking, scrape out the insides and top with salt, marinara, and hot sauce and basil if using. Serve like spaghetti.

4 Store leftovers in the fridge for up to 3 days.

Nutrition Snapshot
Per serving: 112 calories, 3.5 g total fat, 0 g saturated fat, 0 mg cholesterol, 765 mg sodium, 20.5 g carbohydrates, 5 g fiber, 8 g sugar, 2.5 g protein, 19.5% vitamin A, 36.5% vitamin C, 8% calcium, 11.5% iron

Gluten Free

Makes 4 large servings
Prep time 10 minutes
Hands-off cooking time 60 minutes

Indian Zucchini Boats

Just when you thought you'd exhausted all your zucchini recipes to deal with your summer zucchini crop, enter the Indian Zucchini Boats—a new coconutty spin on the garden-grower's special. Enjoy them with Lenticchie all'Arancia *(page 115) and whole wheat naan bread.*

4 medium zucchini, cut in half lengthwise, flesh removed and reserved
2 tsp grapeseed oil
1 small onion, diced
2 medium carrots, shredded
1 tsp ground cumin
¼ tsp turmeric
¼ tsp fennel seeds (optional)
½ tsp salt
½ cup shredded coconut or ¼ cup canned light coconut milk

1 Preheat oven to 375° F.

2 Slice zucchini in half lengthwise, stand each half vertically, and scoop flesh out with a teaspoon using a downward motion. Chop flesh finely and reserve.

3 In a medium-sized skillet over medium-high heat, sauté onion, carrots, zucchini flesh, spices, and salt in oil until onion is translucent, about 8 minutes.

4 Meanwhile, place each zucchini half with scooped-out side up in a large baking or casserole dish that has just enough water to cover bottom, so zucchini doesn't stick.

5 Remove onion mixture from heat and stir in coconut or coconut milk.

6 Divide mixture between zucchini shells and bake, covered, for 30 minutes until the zucchini shells are soft. Serve immediately.

7 Store leftovers in the fridge for up to 3 days.

Nutrition Snapshot
Per serving (2 boats): 110 calories, 7 g total fat, 0 g saturated fat, 0 mg cholesterol, 315 mg sodium, 10 g carbohydrates, 3 g fiber, 5 g sugar, 4 g protein, 79.5% vitamin A, 63.5% vitamin C, 3% calcium, 6.5% iron

Makes 4 servings (2 boats per serving)
Prep time 20 minutes
Hands-off cooking time 30 minutes

Green Beans with Rosemary Pecans and Cranberries

Eating veggies couldn't be easier with Trader Joe's Trimmed and Cleaned Green Beans. You can simply microwave them in the bag and add salt and pepper, or take an extra moment to steam-sauté and add Rosemary Pecans and Cranberries, making them borderline gourmet.

1 (16-oz) bag Trimmed and Cleaned Green Beans, or 1 lb green beans, ends trimmed

¼ cup Rosemary Pecans and Cranberries, finely chopped, or 2 Tbsp each pecans and cranberries (finely chopped) + ½ tsp dried rosemary

1 Microwave green beans for 3-5 minutes according to package instructions, or steam in a medium-sized saucepan with ½ inch water, covered, for 5 minutes.

2 While green beans cook, in a small saucepan over medium-high heat, cook pecans and cranberries in 1 Tbsp water until heated through, about 2 minutes.

3 Divide green beans into 4 portions and top each one with 1 Tbsp pecan cranberry mixture.

4 Store leftovers in the fridge for up to 3 days.

Nutrition Snapshot

Per serving: 74 calories, 2.5 g total fat, 0.5 g saturated fat, 0 mg cholesterol, 9 mg sodium, 12 g carbohydrates, 4 g fiber, 7.5 g sugar, 3 g protein, 13% vitamin A, 31.5% vitamin C, 5.5% calcium, 5.5% iron

G Gluten Free

Makes 4 servings
Prep and cooking time 5 minutes

Chili Lime Sweet Potatoes

My husband who isn't much of a fan of "boring" sweet potatoes, finds this version surprisingly light, tangy, and completely unboring. They go perfectly with Stuffed Peppers *(page 164), or* Minute Mexican *(page 198).*

4 small sweet potatoes, unpeeled, scrubbed, and cut into chunks
Juice of 2 limes, about 3 Tbsp
1 Tbsp agave nectar, maple syrup, or sugar
2 tsp chili powder
2 tsp grapeseed oil, or other vegetable oil
¼ tsp salt

1 Preheat oven to 350° F.

2 Place sweet potatoes in a 9 x 9-inch square baking dish.

3 In a small bowl, whisk together lime juice, agave, chili powder, oil, and salt.

4 Pour juice mixture over sweet potatoes and stir so all potatoes are well-coated.

5 Bake for 40 minutes, until sweet potato chunks are tender.

6 Store leftovers in the fridge for up to 5 days.

Nutrition Snapshot
Per serving: 130 calories, 3.5 g total fat, 0.5 g saturated fat, 0 mg cholesterol, 240 mg sodium, 25 g carbohydrates, 3.5 g fiber, 12.5 g sugar, 2 g protein, 106.5% vitamin A, 33.5% vitamin C, 3.5% calcium, 6.5% iron

G
Gluten Free

Makes 3 servings
Prep time 5 minutes
Hands-off cooking time 40 minutes

Feather-Weight Kale

Kale is a cruciferous veggie powerhouse food that will improve your bone health with its highly absorbable calcium, boost your immune system with its high vitamin A and C content, and basically extend your life for several moons. You absorb over 50% of the calcium in kale and only about 30% from regular milk. Baking kale gives it the light, crispy texture of potato chips. It's snack time!

1 (10-oz) bag cut kale, or 1 bunch kale, stems removed and torn into chunks
1 Tbsp olive oil
½ tsp salt

1 Preheat oven to 350° F.

2 In a 9 x 13-inch baking dish, place kale drizzled with olive oil and sprinkled with salt.

3 Bake for 30 minutes, stirring after 15 minutes and returning to the oven until kale is crisped.

4 Store leftovers in a zipper sealed bag for up to 2 days.

Nutrition Snapshot
Per serving: 66 calories, 5 g total fat, 0.5 g saturated fat, 0 mg cholesterol, 409 mg sodium, 5.5 g carbohydrates, 2 g fiber, 1 g sugar, 2 g protein, 257.5% vitamin A, 64.5% vitamin C, 7% calcium, 5% iron

G
Gluten Free

Makes 3 servings
Prep time 3 minutes
Hands-off cooking time 30 minutes

Sandwiches,
Burgers & Wraps

Pizza Burgers

These burgers are quick to make if you have leftover quinoa. They're delicious eaten as burgers with all the fixin's, or alongside Garlicky Potatoes and Greens *(page 129).*

1 ½ cups cooked quinoa (½ cup dry quinoa cooked with 1 cup water according to package instructions)

1 (15-oz) can kidney beans, drained, rinsed, and mashed

⅓ cup flaxseed meal (ground flaxseeds), or Just Almond Meal

2 Tbsp flaxseed meal or cornstarch whisked with 6 Tbsp filtered water

¼ cup Tomato Basil Marinara or tomato sauce

1 Tbsp spicy brown mustard

2 tsp garlic powder

1 Tbsp dried basil

½ tsp salt

¼ tsp black pepper

1 Tbsp olive oil

1 Mix together all ingredients in a large bowl.

2 In a large skillet over medium-high heat, heat olive oil. Shape mixture into patties and pan-fry on medium-low heat for 10 minutes on each side until lightly browned.

3 Let cool for 5 minutes after cooking to allow the patties to firm up. Enjoy warm.

4 Store leftovers in the fridge for up to 4 days or in the freezer for up to 2 months.

Nutrition Snapshot
Per patty: 93 calories, 3 g total fat, 0 g saturated fat, 0 mg cholesterol, 175 mg sodium, 12 g carbohydrates, 3.5 g fiber, 1 g sugar, 4 g protein, 0% vitamin A, 0% vitamin C, 2% calcium, 6% iron

G Gluten Free

Makes 12 patties
Prep and cooking time 35 minutes

Chicken Salad

The "chicken" in this recipe is tempeh, a fermented soybean product that tops the charts on protein, fiber, and satisfaction. Tempeh has a nutty flavor and delightfully chewy texture. Boiling it eliminates the bitterness found in fermented foods, and also helps prevent the "musical" compounds associated with beans. If you have Tofu Mayo (page 237) made ahead of time, this recipe is a breeze. Enjoy this salad on a bed of greens, or on toasted whole grain bread with lettuce and tomato.

1 (8-oz) pkg Organic 3 Grain Tempeh, broken into chunks and boiled for 8 minutes

2 stalks celery, finely diced (preferably organic)

2 medium carrots, shredded or finely diced

2 Tbsp dill pickle relish

2 scallions (green onions), chopped, or 2 Tbsp finely chopped onion

½ cup Tofu Mayo (page 237)*, or other vegan mayonnaise

3 Tbsp Deli Style Spicy Brown Mustard, or other spicy brown mustard

¼ tsp salt

⅛ tsp black pepper

1 While tempeh boils, combine remaining ingredients in a bowl.

2 Once tempeh has boiled for 8 minutes, drain cooking water using a strainer, and then rinse with cold water.

3 Crumble tempeh into the bowl with other ingredients, and stir to mix all ingredients through.

4 Store leftovers in the fridge for up to 4 days.

Nutrition Snapshot

Per serving: 94 calories, 4.5 g total fat, 0.5 g saturated fat, 0 mg cholesterol, 270 mg sodium, 7 g carbohydrates, 3 g fiber, 1 g sugar, 6.5 g protein, 37.5% vitamin A, 4% vitamin C, 4% calcium, 5.5% iron

*Tofu Mayo: ½ block firm tofu blended with 2 Tbsp brown rice vinegar, 2 Tbsp oil, ½ tsp salt, and a sprinkle of black pepper (Makes 1 ½ cups)

Makes 8 (½-cup) servings
Prep and cooking time 15 minutes
(10 minutes if Tofu Mayo is already made)

Mediterranean Tofu Wrap

This fresh and quickly-prepared wrap is a dance party of healthy flavors. Enjoy it as a quick meal on its own, or with a side salad. Captain Reilly likes this one squashed and heated in a skillet or Panini maker. Hot or cold, you can't go wrong!

1 Habanero Lime Flour Tortilla or whole grain flour tortilla

1 Tbsp hummus, such as Garlic Hummus or *I ♥ Hummus* (page 71)

1 Tbsp Olive Tapenade Spread

2.3 oz (⅓ pkg) Organic Baked Tofu, Savory Flavor, other marinated tofu, or 2 pieces of *The Big Tofu* (page 163), cut into 4 strips

Handful baby lettuce or 1 oz (½ pkg) Organic Microgreens

2 Tbsp Julienne Cut Sun Dried Tomatoes, or other sliced sun dried tomatoes

4 fresh basil leaves

1 With flour tortilla open on a plate, spread hummus and then olive spread evenly over tortilla.

2 Place 4 tofu strips 2 x 2, flat down, and lengthwise. Then top with baby lettuce, sun dried tomatoes, and basil.

3 Wrap the tortilla and secure with a toothpick or foil wrap.

4 Eat within a few hours so olive spread doesn't make the tortilla soggy.

Nutrition Snapshot
Per wrap: 358 calories, 12.5 g total fat, 1.5 g saturated fat, 0 mg cholesterol, 800 mg sodium, 45 g carbohydrates, 6.5 g fiber, 6 g sugar, 17.5 g protein, 41% vitamin A, 31.5% vitamin C, 6.5% calcium, 20.5% iron

Tip Prepare several wraps ahead of time, wrapped in foil, but omitting the olive spread until ready to eat. Store them in the fridge for up to 3 days.

 Use brown rice tortillas

Makes 1 wrap
Prep time 5 minutes

Hot Chickpea Burgers

What I especially love about these electric veggie burgers is that they're easy and cheap to make, they actually stick together, and they aren't made from manipulated soy isolates. Plus, they've got a completely addictive curry flavor. Chickpeas and garbanzo beans are the same creature— use either one. Make a triple recipe and freeze burgers for a rainy day. Serve on a bun with all the fixin's or alongside rice and a heaping side of veggies.

½ small onion, finely chopped

2 small carrots, shredded or finely chopped

2 small celery stalks, shredded or finely chopped (preferably organic)

2 cloves garlic, minced, or 2 cubes frozen Crushed Garlic

1 (15-oz) can garbanzo beans, drained

1 Tbsp reduced-sodium soy sauce

1 ½ tsp curry powder

1 tsp ground cumin

½ tsp ground coriander

⅛ tsp cayenne pepper (optional)

½ tsp salt

¼ cup all-purpose flour

3 Tbsp olive oil

1 In a medium-sized mixing bowl, stir together onion, carrot, celery, garlic, and garbanzo beans. Mash with a potato masher leaving some chunks of beans.

2 Add soy sauce, curry powder, cumin, coriander, cayenne, and salt. Mix thoroughly.

3 Stir in flour and knead the dough by hand so flour is well distributed.

4 Heat oil in a large skillet over medium-high heat. Form dough into patties and cook for 5 minutes on one side and then flip and cook another 3 minutes on the other side until lightly browned.

5 Store leftovers in the fridge for up to 3 days, or in the freezer for up to 2 months.

Nutrition Snapshot
Per patty: 139 calories, 6.5 g total fat, 1 g saturated fat, 0 mg cholesterol, 346 mg sodium, 16.5 g carbohydrates, 4 g fiber, 1 g sugar, 4 g protein, 34.5% vitamin A, 4% vitamin C, 2% calcium, 4.5% iron

 Use Just Almond Meal instead of flour and tamari instead of soy sauce

Makes 7 patties

Prep and cooking time 20 minutes

Veggie Pupusas

These pupusas aren't made of thick hand-made corn tortillas like the traditional Salvadoran version, but they're still pretty bueno and take only a few minutes to make. Creamy hummus and refried beans take the place of high-fat cheese while cilantro, salsa, and spinach elevate the flavors to a new height. Enjoy pupusas with a bowl of Gazpacho à la Shepherd Street *(page 97).*

4 corn tortillas

2 Tbsp hummus, such as Spicy Hummus

2 Tbsp canned low-fat refried beans

2 Tbsp chopped fresh cilantro

4 tsp salsa such as Salsa Verde

2 Tbsp thawed frozen chopped spinach (preferably organic)

1 To make each pupusa, spread 1 Tbsp hummus on 1 tortilla and 1 Tbsp beans on another. Sprinkle 1 Tbsp each cilantro, salsa, and spinach onto the tortilla with the hummus. Put the tortillas together and cook in a dry skillet over medium-high heat for 2 minutes. Flip and cook another 2 minutes on the other side.

2 Repeat with next set of tortillas.

3 Leftovers will last up to a day in the fridge. Reheat in a skillet and enjoy.

Nutrition Snapshot

Per pupusa: 170 calories, 3 g total fat, 0.5 g saturated fat, 0 mg cholesterol, 241 mg sodium, 31 g carbohydrates, 6 g fiber, 0.5 g sugar, 6 g protein, 30.5% vitamin A, 8.5% vitamin C, 8% calcium, 10% iron

G
Gluten Free

Makes 2 pupusas
Prep and cooking time 10 minutes

Broccoli in a Blanket

You've no doubt heard of "pigs in a blanket." Allow me to introduce you to their healthy friends. These wraps are practically instant, colorful, and include raw cruciferous veggies (which effectively shuttle extra hormones out of the body therefore lowering cancer risk, and are also chock full of immune-boosting plant compounds and antioxidants). Does it get any better? This wrap is great for a mini-meal, or accompanied by Keller's Basil Stew *(page 102) for a full-on feast.*

2 whole grain flour tortillas
¼ cup hummus, such as Mediterranean Hummus, or *I* ♥ *Hummus* **(page 71)**
1 ½ cups Organic Broccoli Slaw, or finely chopped or shredded broccoli
1 tomato, sliced
½ cup chopped fresh cilantro or basil
Dash salt and pepper

1 For each wrap, spread 2 Tbsp hummus over one side of the tortilla. Then top it with ¾ cup slaw, ½ diced tomato, ¼ cup chopped cilantro or basil and a dash of salt and pepper.

2 Wrap and roll in foil to eat later, or wrap and chow down immediately.

3 Repeat for the next wrap.

4 Wrapped wraps will keep in the fridge for up to 3 days. Make a bunch at once so there's always some healthy "fast food!"

Nutrition Snapshot
Per serving: 200 calories, 5.5 g total fat, 0.5 g saturated fat, 0 mg cholesterol, 279 mg sodium, 3.5 g carbohydrates, 9.5 g fiber, 3 g sugar, 8.5 g protein, 45.5% vitamin A, 77.5% vitamin C, 6% calcium, 13% iron

G Use brown rice tortillas
Gluten Free

Makes 2 servings
Prep time 5 minutes

The Main Squeeze

Chickpea Mountain Curry

This gorgeous tower of power is one of the heartier skinny dishes. Quinoa is actually a seed that's eaten like a grain, so it's higher in protein and fiber than any whole grain out there. The spiciness of the Thai Green Curry Simmer Sauce will be sure to warm you up on a cold winter day, or have you grabbing an icy seltzer on a hot summer day!

1 cup Organic Red Quinoa, or other quinoa

2 cups filtered water

1 Tbsp olive oil

½ medium onion, diced

3 cloves garlic, chopped (about 3 tsp), or 3 cubes frozen Crushed Garlic

7 oz (~ ⅔ bag) Shredded Carrots, or 3 medium carrots, shredded

2 (15-oz) cans chickpeas or garbanzo beans (they're one and the same!), drained and rinsed

1 cup Wild Arugula Wild Rocket Salad, or other prewashed arugula

1 cup Thai Green Curry Simmer Sauce, or other spicy green curry sauce

Dash hot sauce (optional)

1 In a medium-sized dry pot, toast quinoa by heating it for 4-5 minutes until it crackles vigorously. Add the water, bring to a boil, and then reduce heat to simmer. Cover and cook until all the water is absorbed, about 15 minutes.

2 While the quinoa cooks, in a large skillet over medium-high heat, sauté diced onion and garlic in oil until onion is translucent, about 3 minutes. Add the chickpeas, shredded carrots, ¼ cup arugula, and the simmer sauce. Continue to cook, stirring constantly, until curry starts to bubble, about 4 minutes.

3 Serve over quinoa with additional hot sauce as desired, and topped with a handful of fresh arugula.

Nutrition Snapshot
Per serving: 412 calories, 15 g total fat, 9 g saturated fat, 0 mg cholesterol, 702 mg sodium, 59.5 g carbohydrates, 12 g fiber, 4.5 g sugar, 14 g protein, 76.5% vitamin A, 88% vitamin C, 11% calcium, 28% iron

Makes 6 servings
Prep and cooking time 25 minutes

The Big Tofu

Tofu "steaks" are perfect atop a bed of brown rice or salad, in a stir-fry, or simply on their own. Tofu is high in filling protein, with one serving of this tasty creation containing 25 grams. That's equivalent to 3 ounces of chicken breast, but without any saturated fat or cholesterol. Additionally, each serving of this tofu provides a third of the daily requirement for calcium (daily requirement = 1000 mg)!

2 (15-oz) blocks organic extra firm tofu
3 Tbsp olive oil
⅛ tsp salt
3-4 Tbsp tamari or reduced-sodium soy sauce

1 Press Tofu: Place 6 paper towels on the counter. Drain tofu from package. Place both blocks of tofu on the paper towels, side by side. Place a cutting board or baking sheet on top of tofu. Place 2 or 3 cans of beans or similar weight on top of the cutting board, and let sit for at least 30 minutes. This process gets excess water out of the tofu, allowing it space to soak in other incredible flavors. Tofu is like a flavor sponge!

2 Once tofu is pressed, in an extra large skillet (or 2 medium-sized skillets) heat olive oil over medium-high heat. Slice tofu into 10 slices per block (20 slices total), and place a single layer in the skillet.

3 Sprinkle salt evenly over tofu slices, and cook over medium-low heat, covered with a little room for water to escape, for about 10 minutes.

4 Flip tofu and sprinkle with tamari or soy sauce, and cook for another 5 minutes, turning up the heat to medium-high. Add extra soy sauce or salt as needed for flavor.

5 Store leftovers in the fridge for up to 4 days.

Nutrition Snapshot
Per serving (4 slices): 278 calories, 18 g total fat, 2 g saturated fat, 0 mg cholesterol, 620 mg sodium, 2 g carbohydrates, 0 g fiber, 0 g sugar, 25 g protein, 0% vitamin A, 0% vitamin C, 30% calcium, 20% iron

 **Use tamari instead of soy sauce**

Makes 5 servings
Prep time 15 minutes
Hands-off prep time 30 minutes
for pressing the tofu

Stuffed Peppers

If you have leftover cooked brown rice, this recipe is a cinch and looks totally gourmet. Alternatively, practical cooks can chop the peppers into chunks and line them on the bottom of a baking dish, and then spread the rice mixture over top and bake. Serve that version like lasagna. Same great taste!

3 cups cooked brown rice (1 cup dry brown rice plus 2 cups water—see *Perfect Brown Rice*, page 234)

1 (15-oz) can black beans, drained and rinsed

1 (16-oz) jar of Hot Chipotle Salsa, or about 2 cups of other favorite salsa

4 bell peppers (green, red, orange, and yellow, or a combination), sliced in half length-wise, stem and seeds removed (preferably organic)

¼ cup chopped cilantro for garnish (optional)

1 Preheat oven to 350° F.

2 In a large mixing bowl, combine rice, beans, and salsa. Stuff mixture into pepper halves and place in one or two baking dishes. Cover with aluminum foil and bake until peppers are tender, about 30 minutes.

3 Store leftovers in the fridge for up to 4 days or in the freezer for up to 2 months.

Nutrition Snapshot
Per pepper-half: 163 calories, 1 g total fat, 0 g saturated fat, 0 mg cholesterol, 165 mg sodium, 31.5 g carbohydrates, 5 g fiber, 5.5 g sugar, 5 g protein, 49% vitamin A, 148% vitamin C, 4.5% calcium, 25% iron

G
Gluten Free

Makes 8 pepper-halves (about 4 servings)
Prep time 5 minutes if rice is already cooked
Hands–off cooking time 30 minutes

Racy Risotto

This colorful and creamy coconut curry concoction is a racy twist on the Italian rice staple.
Enjoy it with a fresh side salad or Crave-Worthy Brussels Sprouts *(page 124).*

1 Tbsp Earth Balance Natural Buttery Spread, or other non-hydrogenated margarine

½ medium onion, diced

3 cloves garlic, chopped

2 tsp curry powder

½ cup finely chopped butternut squash

1 red bell pepper, diced (preferably organic)

1 cup frozen or fresh edamame (green soy beans)

½ tsp salt

1 ½ cups dry Arborio rice

1 (14-oz) can light coconut milk

1 ½ cups filtered water

2 Tbsp chopped fresh basil for garnish (optional)

1 In a large saucepan, heat margarine over medium-low heat and sauté onion, garlic, and curry powder until onion is translucent, about 3 minutes.

2 Add butternut squash, red pepper, edamame, and salt; continue to cook on medium-low heat another 5 minutes. Stir in rice.

3 In a separate bowl, combine coconut milk and water.

4 Stir in milk/water mixture to the saucepan with the vegetables, 1 cup at a time, waiting for each cup to be absorbed before adding the next. Continue to cook on medium-low heat, stirring every minute or so until all the liquid has been added and absorbed by the rice, about 18 minutes total.

5 Risotto is done when rice is tender but still has a "bite." Risotto should be creamy. Serve immediately, garnished with basil.

6 Store leftovers in the fridge for up to 4 days.

Nutrition Snapshot
Per serving: 331 calories, 8 g total fat, 3.5 g saturated fat, 0 mg cholesterol, 285 mg sodium, 56.5 g carbohydrates, 5.5 g fiber, 4.5 g sugar, 9.5 g protein, 49.5% vitamin A, 68.5% vitamin C, 4% calcium, 7% iron

Gluten Free

Makes 5 servings
Prep and cooking time 35 minutes

Pesto Pasta

So creamy and flavorful, this one can't be good for you! Oh, but it is. And it only takes a few minutes to prepare. Wow dinner guests and serve this pasta alongside Mango Summer Salad (page 112).

8 oz (½ pkg) organic whole wheat spaghetti

3 cloves garlic

1 lemon, juiced (about ¼ cup lemon juice)

2 Tbsp olive oil

1 medium ripe avocado, pit and peel removed

1 cup fresh basil (a large handful, about 30 leaves)

2 Tbsp filtered water

1 tsp salt

⅛ tsp black pepper

1 Prepare spaghetti according to package instructions.

2 Meanwhile, in a blender or food processor, process garlic, lemon juice, and oil until smooth. Add avocado, basil, water, salt, and pepper; continue to process until creamy.

3 Drain spaghetti and toss with avocado basil mixture. Serve immediately, and finish entire recipe (call up a hungry neighbor!). The avocado will make the pasta dark brown and unappealing as leftovers.

Nutrition Snapshot

Per serving: 350 calories, 15 g total fat, 2 g saturated fat, 0 mg cholesterol, 589 mg sodium, 46.5 g carbohydrates, 8 g fiber, 2 g sugar, 9 g protein, 4% vitamin A, 8.5% vitamin C, 1% calcium, 11% iron

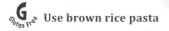 **Use brown rice pasta**

Makes 4 servings

Prep and cooking time 11 minutes

Loafin' Lentils

This meatless meatloaf was adapted from the Ultimate Vegan Lentil Walnut Loaf *by Angela Liddon, MA, of the popular OhSheGlows.com, and she was inspired by Terry Walters'* **Clean Food** *cookbook. It fills the comfort-food category with high marks, and makes a dandy partner for Sesame Greens (page 132). The ingredient list looks a little daunting, but it's actually simple to prepare, and is well worth any extra effort. You'll just wish you had made 2 loaves!*

3 Tbsp flaxseed meal (ground flaxseeds), soaked in ½ cup warm filtered water for 10 minutes until a gel forms, or 3 Tbsp cornstarch dissolved in ½ cup warm water

¾ cup walnuts

1 Tbsp olive oil

3 cloves garlic, minced, or 3 cubes frozen Crushed Garlic

½ onion, finely chopped

1 carrot, shredded

½ green apple, unpeeled and shredded

¼ cup raisins

1 tsp salt

1 tsp dried thyme

⅛ tsp black pepper

2 slices whole grain bread such as Organic Soft Wheat, toasted and then processed in a blender or food processor to make crumbs, or ¾ cup breadcrumbs

1 (17.6-oz) pkg refrigerated Steamed Lentils, or 2 ½ cups cooked lentils

1 Tbsp additional flaxseed meal, or Just Almond Meal

½ cup All Natural Barbeque Sauce, or other barbeque sauce

1 Preheat oven to 350° F.

2 Roast walnuts on a parchment paper lined baking sheet for 6 minutes. Set aside, but keep oven on.

3 Meanwhile, in a large skillet over medium-high heat, heat oil and sauté onion, garlic, and carrot until tender, about 2-3 minutes. Add shredded apple, raisins, salt, thyme, pepper, and walnuts crumbled by hand into the skillet, and sauté another 2 minutes. Pour mixture into the mixing bowl with flaxseed meal and water mixture.

4 Using a food processor, process bread into into breadcrumbs, and then add to the mixing bowl.

5 Process lentils so that ¾ of them are blended smooth, leaving some whole lentils. Add to mixing bowl along with additional tablespoon of flaxseed meal. Stir together. Taste test the mixture now... aren't you excited for the finished product?!

6   Press firmly into a 5 x 9-inch loaf pan. Top with barbeque sauce, spreading it evenly over the loaf.

7   Bake for 45 minutes, and then let cool for 10 minutes before slicing.

8   Store leftovers in the fridge for up to 4 days or in the freezer for up to 2 months.

Nutrition Snapshot

Per serving: 245 calories, 10.5 g total fat, 2 g saturated fat, 0 mg cholesterol, 652 mg sodium, 30.5 g carbohydrates, 8 g fiber, 10.5 g sugar, 9.5 g protein, 20.5% vitamin A, 4.5% vitamin C, 4.5% calcium, 18.5% iron

Use gluten-free bread to make breadcrumbs

Makes 8 servings (8 thick slices)
Prep time 30 minutes
Hands-off cooking time 45 minutes, followed by 10 minutes to cool

Lazy Lasagna

If the word lasagna brings hard labor and never-gonna-happen to mind, think again. This veggie lasagna is quick to construct and doesn't require a knife or cutting board. Build it and toss it in the oven an hour and a half before dinner to avoid the 6:00 PM prep frenzy. And, because a knife isn't required, this recipe is great one to make with kids. Oh, and it's high in fiber, cholesterol-free, and low in saturated fat. What are you waiting for?

1 (16-oz) block organic firm tofu, liquid drained

1 (16-oz) bag frozen chopped spinach, thawed (preferably organic)

1 (8-oz) container vegan cream cheese such as Tofutti Better Than Cream Cheese

1 tsp garlic powder

½ tsp salt

1 (28-oz) can Tuscano Marinara Sauce, or plain tomato sauce

1 (25-oz) jar Organic Tomato Basil Marinara Sauce, or other tomato basil marinara

14.5 oz lasagna noodles (most of a 1-lb box), preferably whole wheat*

1 Preheat oven to 350° F.

2 In a large bowl, crumble tofu and stir in spinach, cream cheese, garlic, and salt.

3 In the bottom of a 9 x 13-inch baking dish, evenly spread half the 28-oz can of marinara or tomato sauce, and then evenly layer with about 5 lasagna noodles (1 of which will probably need to be broken into 2 halves to fit.

4 Spread half the spinach tofu mixture evenly over the lasagna noodles, and cover the spinach tofu mixture with another layer of about 5 lasagna noodles.

5 Pour half the jar of Tomato Basil Marinara evenly over lasagna noodles, and then top that layer of sauce with another layer of noodles (about 5).

6 Spread the other half the spinach tofu mixture evenly over lasagna noodles, and cover with a final layer of lasagna noodles.

7 Top final layer of noodles with the remaining half jar of Tomato Basil Marinara and half can of Tuscano Marinara Sauce, spread evenly over top.

8 Cover tightly with aluminum foil and bake for 1 hour. Stick a knife through the center of the lasagna to make sure the noodles are completely cooked. Let cool for 10 minutes, covered, before serving.

9 Store leftover lasagna in the fridge for up to 3 days, or in individual containers in the freezer for up to 2 months.

Nutrition Snapshot
Per serving: 432 calories, 12.5 g total fat, 2 g saturated fat, 0 mg cholesterol, 1018 mg sodium, 55 g carbohydrates, 13 g fiber, 8.5 g sugar, 19.5 g protein, 101.5% vitamin A, 26.5% vitamin C, 16% calcium, 31% iron

*Whole wheat varieties are generally vegan, whereas regular noodles (such as the ones sold at Trader Joe's) often contain eggs. For a high-fiber, vegan version when whole wheat noodles aren't available, substitute 5 potatoes or 2 large eggplants, thinly sliced lengthwise.

Tip Eliminate the salt or use low-sodium sauce to lower the sodium content of this recipe.

Tip No need to use pre-boiled or no-boil noodles—the regular ones will cook completely in this recipe just fine.

Makes 8 servings
Prep time 20 minutes
Hands-off cooking time 60 minutes, plus 10 minutes to cool

Puerto Rican Rice and Beans

No one makes rice and beans like my favorite Puerto Rican, Rafael Prieto. Here is his secret recipe for a filling and fiber-ific main dish. In Boricua style, serve the rice and beans next to each other, and then mix them while eating.

Rice

1 Tbsp olive oil
1 medium yellow onion, diced
½ tsp black pepper
2 cloves garlic, minced, or 2 cubes frozen Crushed Garlic
1 ½ cups long-grain brown rice
3 cups filtered water

Beans

1 Tbsp olive oil
1 large yellow onion, diced
¼ tsp black pepper
5 cloves garlic, minced, or 5 cubes frozen Crushed Garlic
2 (15-oz) cans kidney beans, undrained
1 tsp cumin
1 green bell pepper, diced (preferably organic)
1 cup pitted black olives (about 25), sliced

Rice

1 In a large pot, sauté onion and black pepper in olive oil over medium-high heat until onion is translucent, about 3 minutes.

2 Add garlic and continue to cook until it starts to brown, about 2 minutes. Add rice, stirring to let it absorb the flavors, about 2 more minutes.

3 Add water and bring to a boil. Cover with a tight lid and reduce heat to simmer. Cook for about 25 minutes, until all the water is absorbed.

Beans

4 While rice cooks, in a separate, medium-sized pot, sauté onion and black pepper in olive oil over medium-high heat until onion is translucent, about 3 minutes.

5 Add garlic and continue to cook until it starts to brown, about 2 minutes.

6 Add remaining ingredients and bring to a boil. Reduce heat to simmer and cook until peppers are tender, about 10 minutes. Serve hot.

7 Store leftovers in the fridge for up to 5 days.

Nutrition Snapshot
Per serving: 447 calories, 9.5 g total fat, 1 g saturated fat, 0 mg cholesterol, 520 mg sodium, 78.5 g carbohydrates, 11.5 g fiber, 4 g sugar, 14.5 g protein, 3% vitamin A, 41% vitamin C, 9.5% calcium, 22% iron

Makes 5 servings
Prep and cooking time 40 minutes

Tempeh Sauté

Tempeh is a fermented soy product and an incredible source of healthy plant protein. Fermented foods like tempeh and miso are naturally high in probiotics which improve digestion and reduce inflammation. Finish this hearty helping off with fresh fruit or Minty Fruit Salad *(page 226).*

1 (8-oz) pkg Organic 3 Grain Tempeh, broken into chunks and boiled for 8 minutes

2 Tbsp toasted sesame oil

1 Tbsp chopped fresh ginger

1 (16-oz) bag frozen Stir-Fry Vegetables, or 5 cups chopped vegetables of choice

½ cup apple juice

1 Tbsp brown rice vinegar

1 pouch (⅓ box) frozen Organic Brown Rice, or 2 cups cooked brown rice
(see *Perfect Brown Rice,* page 234)

3 Tbsp reduced-sodium soy sauce

1 When tempeh is nearly done boiling, heat sesame oil in a large skillet over medium-high heat. Add ginger and then boiled and drained tempeh, and sauté until golden brown, about 5 minutes.

2 Add vegetables, apple juice, and vinegar; continue to cook until vegetables are cooked through, about 8 minutes.

3 While vegetables cook, heat rice according to package directions (3 minutes in microwave).

4 Serve stir-fry over brown rice and top with soy sauce.

5 Store leftovers in the fridge for up to 4 days.

Nutrition Snapshot
Per serving: 496 calories, 19 g total fat, 3 g saturated fat, 0 mg cholesterol, 503 mg sodium, 59 g carbohydrates, 12 g fiber, 4.5 g sugar, 21 g protein, 50% vitamin A, 34% vitamin C, 9% calcium, 22% iron

Note Fermented foods often have a bitter taste. Boiling reduces that bitterness significantly.

Makes 3 servings
Prep and cooking time 25 minutes

Sassy Moussaka

Sass up a lazy Sunday afternoon by making this celebrated Greek dish. While the cooking time is lengthy, the prep is simple, and the first bite will have you dreaming of discus throwing in Athens. Enjoy a hearty serving with a good Pinot Noir, and do the dishes in the morning.

1 eggplant, cut lengthwise into ¼-inch slices, and then let sweat for 10 minutes*

3 Tbsp olive oil, divided

1 medium onion, diced

4 cloves garlic, minced

1 (28-oz) can diced tomatoes

1 tsp oregano

¼ tsp cinnamon

¼ tsp allspice

1 ½ tsp sea salt

½ tsp black pepper

1 large potato, scrubbed, unpeeled, and cut lengthwise into ¼-inch slices

2 zucchini squash, ends removed and cut lengthwise into ¼-inch slices

½ cup chopped fresh parsley for garnish

Béchamel Sauce

2 Tbsp olive oil

⅛ tsp nutmeg

1 cup unsweetened non-dairy milk, such as unsweetened almond milk

12 oz (¾ block) organic firm tofu

1 ½ tsp sea salt

1 Preheat oven to 375° F.

2 In a large skillet over medium-high heat, sauté onion and garlic in 2 Tbsp oil until lightly browned, about 5 minutes. Stir in tomatoes, oregano, cinnamon, allspice, salt, and pepper; continue to cook until heated through, another 3 minutes.

3 Lightly grease the bottom of a 9 x 13-inch baking dish with 1 Tbsp oil. Layer bottom with potato slices, then 1 cup of tomato mixture, eggplant slices, another 1 cup of the tomato mixture, zucchini slices, and the remaining 1 cup of the tomato mixture.

4 Cover tightly with aluminum foil and bake for 60 minutes.

5 Blend together Béchamel Sauce ingredients until smooth. Pour over the baked vegetable mixture and return to the oven, uncovered, to bake for another 20 minutes, until the top is nicely browned.

6 Let sit for 20 minutes and then serve topped with fresh parsley.

7 Store leftovers in the fridge for up to 2 days.

Nutrition Snapshot
Per serving: 193 calories, 11.5 g total fat, 1.5 g saturated fat, 0 mg cholesterol, 1125 mg sodium, 17 g carbohydrates, 4 g fiber, 5 g sugar, 7.5 g protein, 22% vitamin A, 55.5% vitamin C, 11% calcium, 12% iron

* **Tip** Sweating the eggplant gets the bitterness out and softens eggplant for cooking. Slice the eggplant lengthwise and lay the slices flat on a cookie sheet. Sprinkle with salt and let sit for at least 10 minutes. Pat off "sweat" with paper towels.

G Gluten Free

Makes 8 servings
Prep time 20 minutes
Hands-off cooking time 80 minutes

Refrigerator Curry

As long as you have a can of light coconut milk and curry powder on hand, this is a super way to clean out your fridge or freezer. Quinoa cooks in about half the time as brown rice, but this curry could be served over any whole grain of choice, including whole wheat or gluten-free pasta.

1 cup dry quinoa*

2 cups filtered water

1 small onion, diced

2 cloves garlic, minced (about 2 tsp), or 2 cubes frozen Crushed Garlic

1 Tbsp curry powder

1 tsp cumin

½ tsp turmeric

1 (14-oz) can light coconut milk

9 cups chopped raw veggies, or 5 cups frozen veggies**

1 (15-oz) can garbanzo beans, drained and rinsed, or 1 ½ cups cooked beans of choice

3 Tbsp reduced-sodium soy sauce

1 In a medium-sized dry pot, toast the quinoa before adding the water: Heat it for 4-5 minutes until you hear it crackle vigorously. At that point, add the water, bring it to a boil, and then reduce it to a simmer, cover and cook until all the water is absorbed, about 15 minutes.

2 While the quinoa cooks, in a large skillet over medium-high heat, sauté onion and garlic in oil until onion is translucent, about 4 minutes. Add curry powder, cumin, and turmeric; stir for 2 more minutes while flavors combine.

3 Add coconut milk, veggies, and beans; cover and cook until veggies are tender, about 8 minutes (a few more minutes if potatoes are included).

4 Add soy sauce right before serving as it will turn veggies brown.

5 Store leftovers in the fridge for up to 4 days.

Nutrition Snapshot
Per serving (may vary depending on vegetables chosen): 450 calories, 13 g total fat, 5.5 g saturated fat, 0 mg cholesterol, 642 mg sodium, 70 g carbohydrates, 15 g fiber, 7.5 g sugar, 16 g protein, 211.5% vitamin A, 157.5% vitamin C, 10.5% calcium, 23.5% iron

*Look for pre-rinsed quinoa, which guarantees that the bitter soap-like compounds (saponins) have been removed from the quinoa seeds. If you can't find pre-rinsed quinoa, place dry quinoa in a bowl with water, stir it vigorously, and then drain the liquid.

**Examples: 6 chopped carrots = 2 cups, 2 chopped broccoli crowns = 4 cups, 2 chopped zucchini squash = 3 cups.

 Use tamari instead of soy sauce

Makes 4 servings
Prep and cooking time 30 minutes

Roasted Veggie Pizza

Pizza can either be your downfall or your rise to stardom. This one is the latter as it swaps out fatty meats and cheeses with roasted veggies, and sugary sauce with blended fresh tomatoes, high-protein almond meal, and spices. It takes about an hour from start to finish, but the various steps can be spread out throughout the day, or even the day before. Substitute other favorite veggies in the roasted mixture, or simply toss raw veggies on top of the dough and sauce for a super snappy dinner concoction. Serve with a side salad and a Hefeweizen.

Roasted Veggies

2 (14-oz) cans artichoke hearts, drained, and cut in half lengthwise

1 red bell pepper, cut into bite-size pieces (preferably organic)

1 zucchini squash, ends removed and cut into quarter slices

1 Tbsp olive oil

¼ tsp salt

2 cloves garlic, minced (about 2 tsp), or 2 cubes frozen Crushed Garlic

Sauce

½ cup Just Almond Meal, or other almond meal

1 tsp dried basil

1 tsp dried oregano

½ tsp sea salt

2 tomatoes

1 (1-lb) bag 100% Whole Wheat Pizza Dough, plus ½ cup flour for rolling

½ cup sliced black olives for topping

Hot sauce to taste (optional)

1 Preheat oven to 400° F.

2 In a 9 x 13-inch baking dish, place ingredients for Roasted Veggies, stir together, and bake for 40 minutes, until veggies start to brown.

3 Let pizza dough warm to room temperature for 20 minutes.

4 While veggies roast, and dough warms, prepare sauce. In a small dry skillet, toast almond meal, basil, oregano, and salt, stirring until combination starts to brown, about 3 minutes. Set aside to cool.

5   Blend tomatoes in a blender until smooth. Stir into cooled almond meal mixture.

6   Once you're ready to bake the pizza, preheat oven to 425° F, and roll out dough on a floured surface into a 12-inch circular or square pie. Delicately place on a warm pizza stone or lightly oiled baking sheet.

7   With a spatula, spread sauce over dough and top with roasted veggies and olives.

8   Bake for 15 minutes, until crust starts to brown. Serve topped with hot sauce if desired.

9   You won't have leftovers, but just in case, they'll last in the fridge for up to 3 days.

Nutrition Snapshot
Per slice: 238 calories, 8 g total fat, 0.5 g saturated fat, 0 mg cholesterol, 613 mg sodium, 35.5 g carbohydrates, 7.5 g fiber, 2.5 g sugar, 8.5 g protein, 13.5% vitamin A, 37.5% vitamin C, 8.5% calcium, 18% iron

G Gluten Free

Makes 8 slices
Prep and cooking time 60 minutes

Cannellini Ratatouille

Ratatouille originated near Nice, France and comes from the French word "touiller," which means to toss food. The original version didn't include eggplant, just summer vegetables including zucchini, bell peppers, and tomatoes. This edition uses optional eggplant and mushrooms plus carrots and cannellini beans, and is served over toasted whole wheat couscous for a complete meal. Enjoy it with a fresh green salad or all on its own.

1 Tbsp olive oil

1 small onion, diced

3 cloves garlic, minced, or 3 cubes frozen Crushed Garlic

1 ½ tsp each dried oregano, basil, and thyme

⅛ tsp black pepper

1 tsp salt

1 (28-oz) can diced tomatoes

2 green bell peppers, cut into bite-size pieces (preferably organic)

1 red bell pepper, cut into bite-size pieces (preferably organic)

3 zucchini squash, cut into bite-size pieces

2 carrots, unpeeled, cut into coins

5 mushrooms, sliced (optional)

1 eggplant, unpeeled, cut into chunks (optional)

1 (15-oz) can cannellini beans, drained and rinsed

2 cups whole wheat couscous

2 cups filtered water

½ cup chopped fresh parsley or basil (optional)

1 In a large pot, sauté onion, garlic, spices, pepper, and salt in oil over medium-high heat until onion is translucent, about 3 minutes. Add diced tomatoes and remaining vegetables and bring to a boil, reduce heat to simmer and cook, covered, until vegetables are tender, about 5-10 minutes.

2 While vegetables cook, in a medium-sized dry pot, toast couscous by heating it over-medium-high heat for 4-5 minutes until it starts to brown. Immediately remove from heat, add water, and cover. Let sit until all the water is absorbed, about 5 minutes.

3 Once vegetables are tender, remove from heat and stir in cannellini beans. Cover and let sit 2 minutes. Serve over couscous topped with chopped fresh parsley or basil, if using.

4 Store leftovers in the fridge for up to 4 days.

Nutrition Snapshot

Per serving: 380 calories, 4 g total fat, 0.5 g saturated fat, 0 mg cholesterol, 840 mg sodium, 72 g carbohydrates, 16 g fiber, 11.5 g sugar, 14.5 g protein, 111% vitamin A, 153% vitamin C, 9% calcium, 15% iron

G Gluten Free

Serve over rice, quinoa, or brown rice pasta

Makes 6 servings
Prep and cooking time 20 minutes

Eight-Minute Meals

Chili Cook-Off

Everyone's got a favorite chili recipe, but this one is soon to become your favorite and takes less than 10 minutes to prepare. Serve alongside a handful of multigrain chips and a salad of prewashed mixed greens with bottled Light Champagne Vinaigrette for the total package. If you have more time, fire up some Hot Pants Cornbread *(page 229).*

2 tsp olive oil

1 small onion, diced

2 cubes frozen Crushed Garlic, or 2 tsp minced garlic (about 2 cloves)

2 Tbsp chili powder

1 tsp cumin

1 (28-oz) can diced tomatoes

1 large green bell pepper, cut into bite-size pieces (preferably organic)

1 (15-oz) can kidney beans, drained and rinsed

1 (15-oz) can black beans, drained and rinsed

2 cups frozen Roasted Corn or other frozen corn kernels

Juice of 1 lime (optional)

Hot sauce, chopped fresh cilantro, or avocado chunks for garnish (optional)

1 In a large soup pot over medium-high heat, sauté onion, garlic, chili powder, and cumin in oil until onion is translucent, about 3 minutes.

2 Turn heat to high and add tomatoes, pepper, beans, and corn; continue to cook, covered, until heated through, about 3 more minutes.

3 Squeeze lime over chili and top with hot sauce, fresh cilantro, or avocado chunks if desired.

4 Store leftovers in the fridge for up to 5 days or as individual servings in the freezer for up to 2 months.

Nutrition Snapshot
Per cup: 205 calories, 2 g total fat, 0 g saturated fat, 0 mg cholesterol, 438 mg sodium, 38.5 g carbohydrates, 9 g fiber, 7.5 g sugar, 9.5 g protein, 28% vitamin A, 65.5% vitamin C, 6% calcium, 34.5% iron

Makes 7 (1-cup) servings
Prep and cooking time 8 minutes

Sage White Bean Spaghetti

This snappy combo is full of flavor and is a great main dish alongside Blink-of-An-Eye Green Salad *(page 108). Save a few minutes cooking the noodles by skipping the pre-boiling step and using less water. Wham, pow, chow!*

8 oz (½ pkg) spaghetti (preferably whole wheat) or angel hair pasta noodles

1 Tbsp olive oil

5 cubes frozen Crushed Garlic

15 leaves fresh sage, finely chopped, or 2 Tbsp dried sage

½ tsp salt

2 (15-oz) cans white kidney beans (cannellini beans), drained and rinsed

1 Place spaghetti or angel hair pasta in 4 cups cold water, cover, and bring to a boil, about 3 minutes. Remove cover and continue to boil, stirring occasionally until noodles are cooked to desired consistency, 3-5 more minutes.

2 While noodles cook, heat oil in a medium-sized skillet. Add garlic, sage, and salt and sauté 2 minutes, until garlic is golden brown. Add beans and cook another 3 minutes, just enough to heat through.

3 Drain noodles, and serve topped with white beans.

4 Store leftovers in the fridge for up to 3 days.

Nutrition Snapshot

Per serving: 379 calories, 4 g total fat, 0.5 g saturated fat, 0 mg cholesterol, 417 mg sodium, 66.5 g carbohydrates, 22.5 g fiber, 1.5 g sugar, 20 g protein, 1% vitamin A, 2.5% vitamin C, 21.5% calcium, 25.5% iron

*Spaghetti and other pasta noodles take varying times to cook depending on type (whole wheat or white), thickness, and desired firmness. Spaghetti takes about 8 minutes whereas angel hair pasta takes about 6 minutes.

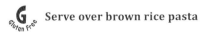 Serve over brown rice pasta

Makes 4 servings
Prep and cooking time 8 minutes*

Beijing Express

This one-dish Asian invasion is far easier, faster, and healthier than picking up the phone and ordering Chinese. Keep these ingredients on hand for a lickety-split go-to meal. To reduce the sodium content of this meal, use only 1 of the sauce packets that comes with the frozen veggies.

2 (16-oz) bags frozen Asian Vegetables with Beijing Style Soy Sauce, or other stir-fry veggies each with ¼ cup stir-fry sauce

2 (8-oz) pkgs Chicken-Less Strips, Beef-Less Strips, or 1 of each, or other meatless strips

1 (7.4-oz) pkg Fully Cooked Organic Brown Rice, or 1½ cups cooked brown rice

1 In a large skillet, place veggies, sauce, meatless strips, and rice and cook, covered, over medium-high heat until vegetables are hot, about 8 minutes.

2 Serve immediately and store leftovers in the fridge for up to 4 days.

Nutrition Snapshot
Per serving: 370 calories, 3 g total fat, 0 g saturated fat, 0 mg cholesterol, 1231 mg sodium, 45 g carbohydrates, 7 g fiber, 15.5 g sugar, 37.5 g protein, 69% vitamin A, 55.5% vitamin C, 13% calcium, 64% iron

Makes 4 servings
Prep and cooking time 8 minutes

Pressure's On Pasta

When it's 6:22 PM and you haven't even started dinner, grab these four ingredients and 2 cooking pots, and you'll be able to sit down by 6:30. The "meaty" sauce will fill you up fast after a long day, and its 11 grams of fiber help you easily meet your 40-gram daily goal. Now that's fast food even a dietitian can get behind!

3 cups dry small regular pasta (such as elbows or shells)*
1 (26-oz) jar Tomato Basil Marinara, or other marinara sauce
1 (17.6-oz) pkg refrigerated Steamed Lentils
2 cups frozen chopped spinach (preferably organic)

1 In a large covered pot, bring pasta and 6 cups water to a boil, about 3 minutes. Remove cover and continue to cook until pasta reaches desired consistency, about 3 more minutes. Drain.

2 Meanwhile, in a medium-sized pot, place marinara, lentils, and spinach and cook on medium-high heat, covered, until edges come to a boil, about 4 minutes.

3 Stir sauce, turn heat down to medium-low, and continue to cook another 2 minutes until heated through.

4 Serve each cup of cooked pasta topped with 1 cup sauce.

5 Store leftovers in the fridge for up to 5 days or as individual servings in the freezer for up to 2 months.

Nutrition Snapshot
Per serving: 384 calories, 5.5 g total fat, 0.5 g saturated fat, 0 mg cholesterol, 778 mg sodium, 67 g carbohydrates, 11 g fiber, 10 g sugar, 17 g protein, 61.5% vitamin A, 15% vitamin C, 6.5% calcium, 30% iron

*Note Whole wheat pasta takes a tad longer to cook than regular, so if you have a few extra minutes, use a whole wheat variety and score 6 more grams of fiber per cup.

Use Organic Fully Cooked
Brown Rice in place of pasta

Makes 6 servings
Prep and cooking time 8 minutes

Lazy Lentils

Fortify a can of lentil soup with extra veggies, and you've got a nutritionist-approved value meal in even less than 8 minutes! Serve this dish with a chunk of whole grain bread or a handful of multigrain crackers. Dinner's served!

2 (14.5-oz) cans Organic Lentil Vegetable Soup
2 cups Organic Foursome frozen vegetables, or other mixed vegetables
2 servings multigrain bread or crackers of choice (optional)

1 In a medium-sized soup pot over medium-high heat, heat soup contents and veggies, covered, until veggies are tender, about 5 minutes.

2 That's it!

Nutrition Snapshot
Per serving: 334 calories, 7 g total fat, 1 g saturated fat, 0 mg cholesterol, 1130 mg sodium, 54.5 g carbohydrates, 14.5 g fiber, 4.5 g sugar, 15 g protein, 119.5% vitamin A, 39% vitamin C, 11% calcium, 33% iron

Serve with rice crackers, such as Savory Thins

Makes 2 servings
Prep and cooking time 6 minutes

Minute Mexican

With little chopping and quick construction, this household standby is always a hit.
Add chopped onions, lettuce, or even sautéed veggies if you're feeling wild.

4 whole wheat or multigrain tortillas

1 (16-oz) can Refried Black Beans with Jalapeño Peppers, or other low-fat refried beans

2 tomatoes, diced

1 avocado, pit removed and cut into chunks

1 lime, sliced into 4 wedges

1 cup Double Roasted Salsa, or other salsa

½ cup chopped cilantro (optional)

Hot sauce to taste (optional)

1 Warm beans in a microwave-safe dish for 1 minute. (Or, heat in a small saucepan over medium heat, stirring, until bubbly, about 3 minutes.)

2 Spread ½ cup beans over each tortilla, and heat in a medium skillet over medium-low heat until tortilla starts to brown, about 2 minutes. Slide each tortilla from skillet to plate.

3 Sprinkle each tortilla with ¼ of the tomato, ¼ avocado, lime juice, ¼ cup salsa, 2 Tbsp chopped cilantro, and dash hot sauce if using. Fold in half, grab a napkin, and chow! Repeat 3 times for additional tortillas.

4 Leftovers will get soggy once the salsa has been added, so start out with one burrito per person and go from there.

Nutrition Snapshot
Per serving: 322 calories, 8.5 g total fat, 1 g saturated fat, 0 mg cholesterol, 768 mg sodium, 51.5 g carbohydrates, 14 g fiber, 2 g sugar, 12.5 g protein, 11% vitamin A, 35% vitamin C, 7% calcium, 24% iron

*Note Use 4 skillets and 4 burners, and make all 4 at the same time!

Use brown rice tortillas or twice as many corn tortillas

Makes 4 servings
Prep and cooking time
6-8 minutes per tortilla*

Sweet Finishes
& Baked Goods

Zeus Mousse

This version of the famous high-fat French delicacy has one-third the fat and calories, but all the flavor. Enjoy it with fresh fruit in a fancy glass while listening to French music, and you'll feel like you're desserting along the Seine!

1 (12-oz) bag semi-sweet chocolate chips
8 oz vanilla almond milk, or other vanilla non-dairy milk
1 (15-oz) block organic firm tofu, drained
12 strawberries, cherries, or raspberries for garnish

1 Place chocolate chips and almond milk in a microwave safe bowl and microwave for about 1 minute, until chips are soft. Let sit another 2 minutes to let the milk fully melt the chips.

2 Place melted chips, milk, and drained tofu in a blender or food processor and blend until creamy. Chill for 1 hour either in the blender or processor or individual cups. Garnish with fruit and enjoy!

3 Store in the fridge for up to 4 days or in popsicle molds in the freezer for up to 1 month.

Nutrition Snapshot

Per serving (½ cup, including strawberries): 181 calories, 11 g total fat, 5 g saturated fat, 0 mg cholesterol, 14.5 mg sodium, 21.5 g carbohydrates, 0.5 g fiber, 17 g sugar, 6 g protein, 1% vitamin A, 11.5% vitamin C, 6% calcium, 4.5% iron

Per DOUBLE Serving (not necessarily recommended, but these things happen): 362 calories, 22 g total fat, 1 g fiber, 34 g sugar, 12 g protein

Option for kids or kids-at-heart: Freeze mousse overnight in rinsed-out yogurt containers with a popsicle stick in the middle. Enjoy the rich popsicle treats for up to a month!

G
Gluten Free

Makes 12 (½-cup) servings
Prep time 5 minutes
Hands-off prep time 1 hour for chilling

Orange Chocolate Cake

This recipe idea came to me while I was making a batch of Shamrock Smoothies (page 38). I was eating a piece of dark chocolate and licked the spoon containing orange juice concentrate for the smoothies. At first I said "whoops," and then I grabbed my recipe notebook! Here's the cake that resulted, which evokes a heavenly chocolate and orange taste marriage. It's so simple that it may become your go-to chocolate dessert.

1 ¾ cups all-purpose flour

½ cup sugar

¼ cup cocoa

1 tsp baking soda

½ tsp salt

½ cup orange juice concentrate, thawed

⅓ cup vegetable oil

2 tsp vanilla

1 tsp apple cider vinegar

½ cup plus 1 Tbsp filtered water

1 Tbsp powdered sugar, or ¼ cup thin vanilla frosting to top

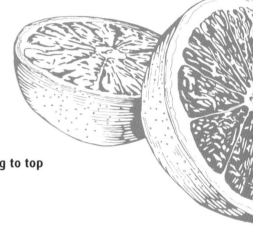

1 Preheat oven to 350° F.

2 Sift dry ingredients together (minus the powdered sugar). Add thawed OJ concentrate (use a microwave for quick thawing) and remaining wet ingredients, stirring until smooth.

3 Pour batter into lightly oiled 9 x 9-inch baking dish and bake for 30-35 minutes, until a toothpick inserted in center comes out clean. Let cake sit 10 minutes before sprinkling with powdered sugar (use a sifter for a delicate, and evenly topped cake), or drizzling with vanilla frosting.

Nutrition Snapshot
Per serving: 225 calories, 8 g total fat, 1 g saturated fat, 0 mg cholesterol, 399 mg sodium, 36 g carbohydrates, 2 g fiber, 17 g sugar, 3 g protein, 0.5% vitamin A, 31% vitamin C, 1% calcium, 7% iron

Makes 9 servings
Prep time 10 minutes
Hands-off cooking time 35 minutes

Chocolate Things

They're not cake, they're not cookies, and they're not bars. They're just THINGS, and they are unbelievable!

2 cups all-purpose flour

1 tsp baking powder

½ tsp baking soda

½ tsp salt

½ cup sugar

¼ cup melted Earth Balance Natural Buttery Spread, or other non-hydrogenated margarine

¼ cup maple syrup

3 tsp vanilla

¾ cup non-dairy milk, such as almond milk

½ cup semi-sweet chocolate chips

1 Preheat oven to 350° F.

2 Sift dry ingredients together. Add wet ingredients and stir until creamy. Stir in chocolate chips.

3 Lightly oil a 9 x 9-inch baking dish. Pour batter into dish and spread evenly. Bake for 30 minutes or until a toothpick inserted in center comes out clean. Let cool 5 minutes before digging in (if you can wait that long).

4 Freeze individual portions for up to 1 month to prevent overeating.

Nutrition Snapshot
Per serving: 270 calories, 7.5 g total fat, 3 g saturated fat, 0 mg cholesterol, 311 mg sodium, 46.5 g carbohydrates, 2 g fiber, 24 g sugar, 3.5 g protein, 1% vitamin A, 0% vitamin C, 5.5% calcium, 12% iron

Makes 9 servings
Prep time 10 minutes
Hands-off cooking time 30 minutes

Zucchini Bread

Zucchini bread and pumpkin pie are the pioneers of sneaky vegetable dishes. This bread is a wonderful breakfast bread, snack, or dessert, and can be made into muffins or cupcakes—just reduce the cooking time to 25 minutes. Celebrate history, and cheers to zucchini bread!

2 cups whole wheat flour

1 cup sugar

2 tsp cinnamon

¼ tsp nutmeg

½ tsp salt

½ tsp baking soda

¼ cup applesauce

¼ cup melted Earth Balance Natural Buttery Spread, or other non-hydrogenated margarine

1 Tbsp vanilla extract

2 Tbsp flaxseed meal (ground flaxseeds) or cornstarch whisked with 6 Tbsp filtered warm water

2 cups shredded zucchini (about 1 medium zucchini, shredded)

1 Preheat oven to 350° F.

2 Mix together dry ingredients.

3 Add wet ingredients—minus the zucchini—until mixed through. Stir in zucchini and add up to ¼ cup of filtered water, if needed, to further moisten batter. Pour batter into a lightly greased and lightly floured 9 x 5-inch loaf pan.

4 Bake for 55-60 minutes, or until a toothpick inserted in center comes out clean. Slice and serve.

5 Leftover zucchini bread can be sliced and stored in individual bags in the freezer for quick breakfasts or sweet snacks.

Nutrition Snapshot
Per serving: 218 calories, 5 g total fat, 1.5 g saturated fat, 0 mg cholesterol, 230 mg sodium, 39 g carbohydrates, 3.5 g fiber, 21 g sugar, 4 g protein, 1% vitamin A, 8.5% vitamin C, 1% calcium, 6% iron

Makes 10 slices **Prep time** 15 minutes
Hands-off cooking time 55 minutes

Gingerbread

This gingerbread is simple to prepare (despite the long list of ingredients!) and a wonderful low-fat treat any time of year. Blackstrap molasses not only makes it deliciously dark, but is also a fantastic source of iron. If you're feeling extra daring, you can add a shredded carrot to the recipe. Turn this recipe into pancakes by replacing the water with 2 cups non-dairy milk, and then using the vegetable oil for cooking in a large skillet. Add fruit sauce or maple syrup. Delectable!

½ cup raisins

¾ cup sugar

½ tsp salt

2 tsp cinnamon

1 tsp ground ginger

¾ tsp nutmeg

¼ tsp ground cloves

1 ½ cups filtered water

2 cups all-purpose flour

1 tsp baking soda

1 tsp baking powder

¼ cup blackstrap molasses or pure maple syrup

2 Tbsp vegetable oil or melted Earth Balance Natural Buttery Spread or similar non-hydrogenated margarine

¼ cup fruit jam heated with 3 Tbsp filtered water, or 1 Tbsp powdered sugar as topping (optional)

1 Combine raisins, sugar, salt, cinnamon, ginger, nutmeg, cloves, and water in a large saucepan and bring to a boil. Boil for 2 minutes, then remove from heat and cool completely, either in the refrigerator for 15 minutes, or in the freezer for about 5 minutes.

2 Preheat oven to 350° F.

3 Stir together flour, baking soda, and baking powder. Add to the cooled raisin mixture along with molasses and vegetable oil or melted margarine; stir thoroughly.

4 Spread batter in a lightly oiled 9-inch round pan and bake for 30 minutes, or until a toothpick inserted in center comes out clean.

5 Let gingerbread cool completely before slicing or topping with thinned fruit jam or sugar, if using.

6 Cover cooled leftovers with foil or transfer to an airtight container. Store sliced gingerbread in individual zipper bags in the freezer for up to a month.

Nutrition Snapshot
Per slice (including thinned fruit topping): 269 calories, 2.5 g total fat, 1 g saturated fat, 0 mg cholesterol, 400 mg sodium, 59 g carbohydrates, 1.5 g fiber, 28.5 g sugar, 3.5 g protein, 0% vitamin A, 0.5% vitamin C, 12.5% calcium, 17.5% iron

Makes 8 large slices
Prep time 20 minutes
Hands-off cooking time 30 minutes

Sesame Cherry Chewies

These delightful creations come from Ami Karnosh, certified nutritionist and founder of Yummy Mummy Cookies in Seattle, Washington. They're incredibly simple to make, powerfully satisfying, and each ingredient supports a healthy body. More dessert, please!

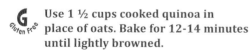

1 ¼ cups old-fashioned rolled oats

¾ cup creamy almond butter or peanut butter

½ cup sesame seeds (nearly 1 whole 2.2-oz jar)

¼ tsp salt (omit if almond or peanut butter are salted)

½ cup agave nectar or maple syrup

½ cup chopped dried cherries or dried cranberries

1 Preheat oven to 375° F.

2 Mix together all ingredients in a bowl. Drop 1 ½-inch balls onto a cookie sheet. Lightly press cookies to flatten slightly.

3 Bake 8-10 minutes, until very lightly browned. Watch carefully as these cookies can burn quickly.

4 Cool and store in an airtight container for up to 2 weeks or freeze for up to 3 months.

Nutrition Snapshot

Per cookie (¹/₁₆ th of recipe): 167 calories, 9 g total fat, 1 g saturated fat, 0 mg cholesterol, 59 mg sodium, 19.5 g carbohydrates, 2.5 g fiber, 11.5 g sugar, 4.5 g protein, 2.5% vitamin A, 0.5% vitamin C, 8.5% calcium, 8% iron

G Gluten Free **Use 1 ½ cups cooked quinoa in place of oats. Bake for 12-14 minutes until lightly browned.**

Makes 16-20 cookies

Prep and cooking time 20 minutes

Strawberry Lemon Tart

This far-out dessert started as a cheese-less cheesecake and morphed into a ridiculously delicious tart. It will wow you again and again.

Cinnamon Graham Crust

3 cups (about 90) Cinnamon Schoolbook Cookies, or about 8 oz graham crackers

⅓ cup Earth Balance Natural Buttery Spread, or other non-hydrogenated margarine

1 Preheat oven to 350° F.

2 In a blender or food processor, blend cookies until they're crumbs. Add margarine and process until evenly mixed.

3 Press mixture into the bottom and sides of a 9-inch round pie pan so the edges come nearly to the top. The filling will only reach halfway up the pie pan, so the crust doesn't need to come precisely to the top.

4 Bake crust for 5 minutes, and let cool completely before adding filling and baking further.

Lemony Filling and Strawberry Topping

1 (8-oz) container Tofutti Better Than Cream Cheese, or other non-dairy cream cheese

¾ cup sugar

2 tsp vanilla

3 Tbsp lemon juice

2 Tbsp cornstarch

10 medium strawberries, stems removed and sliced lengthwise (preferably organic)

1 Blend together cream cheese, sugar, vanilla, lemon juice, and cornstarch until smooth.

2 Pour filling into cooled crust and bake for 35 minutes, until the filling puffs up completely and has a golden glimmer. Let cool in the fridge for about 1 hour to solidify the filling. (If you can't wait, at least let it cool to room temperature, and then top with strawberries. It will be a bit gooey, but still incredibly delicious.)

3 Arrange sliced strawberries on top and enjoy right away.

4 Store leftover slices (if there are any) in the fridge for up to 5 days.

Nutrition Snapshot

Per slice: 208 calories, 10 g total fat, 5 g saturated fat, 0 mg cholesterol, 169 mg sodium, 27.5 g carbohydrates, 1 g fiber, 26 g sugar, 2 g protein, 0% vitamin A, 11% vitamin C, 0% calcium, 2.5% iron

Makes 12 slices
Prep time 20 minutes
Hands-off cooking time 35 minutes plus 1 hour for chilling

Raw Mango Pie

This nifty raw pie is a creation by Janet McKee, a Holistic Health Counselor in Pittsburgh, Pennsylvania. It's perfect in the summer when mangos are in season and the days are hot.

1 ½ cups Just Almond Meal

6 Fancy Medjool Dates, soaked in warm filtered water for 10 minutes

⅛ tsp sea salt

4 mangos, seed removed and cut into chunks, or 1 (24-oz) bag frozen Mango Chunks, thawed

2 bananas

1 While dates soak, blend mangos and 1 banana until smooth. Set aside.

2 In a food processor or blender, process almond meal, dates, and salt until well-blended. Press into a freezer-safe pie pan or baking dish, or 8 individual dessert cups.*

3 Pour mango-banana mixture into pie pan, baking dish, or individual cups and freeze for about 6 hours, until firm.

4 Let pie sit about 30 minutes at room temperature before serving.

Nutrition Snapshot
Per servings: 259 calories, 11.5 g total fat, 1 g saturated fat, 0 mg cholesterol, 40 mg sodium, 37.5 g carbohydrates, 6 g fiber, 27.5 g sugar, 6.5 g protein, 13% vitamin A, 45% vitamin C, 7% calcium, 6% iron

*Pie may be a bit sticky and tricky to serve from the pie pan, so use individual dessert cups if you have them.

G
Gluten Free

Makes 8 servings
Prep time 15 minutes
Hands–off prep time 6 hours to freeze plus 30 minutes to sit at room temp before serving

Squash Drop Cookies

My neighbor, Sara Duke, modified the old Better Homes and Gardens New Cookbook version of Pumpkin Drop Cookies by replacing the raisins with chocolate chips to guarantee getting more colorful beta-carotene goodness into her kids. This version is an even skinnier one using whole wheat flour, flaxseed meal instead of eggs, less sugar, and canned pumpkin (a squash) OR butternut squash (also a squash). If it's not squash season, you can use 2 medium sweet potatoes, peeled, cooked, and mashed instead. Mash, drop, and inhale!

1 Tbsp flaxseed meal (ground flaxseeds), soaked in 3 Tbsp warm filtered water for 10 minutes until it forms a gel, or 1 Tbsp cornstarch dissolved in 2 Tbsp warm water

2 cups whole wheat flour

1 tsp baking powder

1 Tbsp cinnamon

½ tsp baking soda

1 tsp ground nutmeg

⅓ cup Earth Balance Natural Buttery Spread, or other non-hydrogenated margarine, softened to room temp

¾ cup packed brown sugar, or ½ cup granulated sugar + ¼ cup agave nectar

1 (15-oz) can cooked pumpkin, or 1 ½ cups cooked and mashed butternut squash (24 oz cubed or peeled squash, cooked and mashed)

2 tsp vanilla

1 cup semi-sweet chocolate chips or raisins

1 Preheat oven to 375° F.

2 While flaxseed meal soaks, stir together flour, baking powder, cinnamon, soda and nutmeg in a medium-sized mixing bowl.

3 Combine margarine, brown sugar or granulated sugar plus agave, squash, vanilla, and flaxseed water mixture in a separate, large mixing bowl.

4 Add dry ingredients to wet mixture, and stir until well combined. Stir in chocolate chips.

5 Drop from a tablespoon 1 inch apart onto a greased cookie sheet. Bake for 8-10 minutes. Cool on a wire rack. Best when eaten warm, not hot, fresh from oven.

6 Store in an airtight container for 3 days or in the freezer for up to 3 months.

Nutrition Snapshot

Per cookie: 113 calories, 4.5 g total fat, 2 g saturated fat, 0 mg cholesterol, 64 mg sodium, 19 g carbohydrates, 1.5 g fiber, 12 g sugar, 1.5 g protein, 6% vitamin A, 2% vitamin C, 2% calcium, 2.5% iron

Makes 30 cookies
Prep time 12 minutes
Hands-off cooking time 10 minutes

Raspberry Applesauce

Fresh-cooked applesauce is a beautiful fall treat that can also find a happy home atop oatmeal or sorbet. Raspberries glorify the apples with their high antioxidant and antimicrobial content working to prevent cancer and bacterial growth. Plus, forget the chicken noodle soup when you're feeling crummy, one serving of this hot applesauce contains one-third the daily supply of sickness-fighting vitamin C. In addition, raspberries are one of nature's top-10 highest fiber foods. Basically, you'll be healthier by opting FOR dessert in this case!

3 tart apples such as Granny Smith, unpeeled, cored, and cut into chunks (preferably organic)

2 cups raspberries (fresh or frozen)

1 Tbsp cinnamon

2 Tbsp filtered water

1 Place all ingredients in a medium pot, and cook over medium-low heat, covered, until apples are soft, about 15 minutes. Remove from heat and mash with a fork or potato masher, or serve chunky.

2 Store leftovers in the fridge for up to 5 days, or in the freezer for 2 months.

Nutrition Snapshot
Per serving: 114 calories, 1.5 g total fat, 0 g saturated fat, 0 mg cholesterol, 1 mg sodium, 30.5 g carbohydrates, 9 g fiber, 17 g sugar, 0.5 g protein, 1.5% vitamin A, 32.5% vitamin C, 3.5% calcium, 5.5% iron

Gluten Free

Makes 4 servings
Prep time 20 minutes

Xtreme Apple Muffins (or Cupcakes!)

Ever wondered how to take a quick bread mix and make it healthier? Use flaxseed meal or cornstarch instead of eggs, non-dairy milk instead of regular milk, and add veggies or fruits. This upgrade will guarantee all the taste but zero cholesterol, less total fat and saturated fat, and a whole lot more fiber. These muffins are so tasty, they can even be cupcaked. Frost the muffins with vanilla icing and top with sprinkles. A Happier Birthday!

1 (16-oz) pkg Spiced Apple Bread Mix

2 Tbsp flaxseed meal (ground flaxseeds), soaked in 6 Tbsp warm filtered water for 10 minutes until it forms a gel, or 2 Tbsp cornstarch dissolved in ¼ cup warm water

¼ cup melted Earth Balance Natural Buttery Spread, or other non-hydrogenated margarine

1 cup unsweetened rice milk, or other unsweetened non-dairy milk

1 large Granny Smith or other tart apple, unpeeled, shredded or finely diced (preferably organic)

1　Preheat oven to 375° F.

2　Combine flaxseed meal and warm water in a small bowl. Set aside for 10 minutes.

3　Meanwhile, in a large bowl, combine bread mix with melted margarine and milk.

4　Lightly oil 18-cup muffin pan, or line pan with paper baking cups.

5　Add flaxseed meal water mixture and shredded apple to batter, and stir together.

6　Portion batter ⅔ full into each muffin cup.

7　Bake for 28-30 minutes, or until a toothpick inserted in center comes out clean.

8　Let cool for 10 minutes before removing from pan (if you can wait that long).

Nutrition Snapshot
Per muffin: 119 calories, 3 g total fat, 1 g saturated fat, 0 mg cholesterol, 281 mg sodium, 22.5 g carbohydrates, 1.5 g fiber, 11 g sugar, 1.5 g protein, 0.5% vitamin A, 0.5% vitamin C, 3% calcium, 4.5% iron

Makes 18 muffins
Prep time 15 minutes
Hands-off cooking time 28-30 minutes, plus 10 minutes to cool

Option Ice with vanilla frosting and top with sprinkles for apple cupcakes!

Reilly Irish Soda Bread

This recipe emigrated from County Longford, Ireland, and has existed up until now on a tattered piece of notebook paper treasured by my father-in-law, Michael Reilly. Irish soda bread is traditionally a simple breakfast bread or afternoon accompaniment to a cup of Irish breakfast tea, but it also makes a lovely dessert. This version has evolved slightly using soy "buttermilk" to further healthify generations of Reillys. Cheers!

Dough
1 ⅓ cups original soy milk

1 Tbsp plus 1 tsp lemon juice or vinegar

3 cups all-purpose flour

3 Tbsp sugar

3 tsp baking powder

½ tsp baking soda

½ tsp salt

½ cup packed raisins or currants

⅓ cup melted Earth Balance Natural Buttery Spread, or other non-hydrogenated margarine

Glaze
3 Tbsp hot filtered water

3 Tbsp sugar

1 Preheat oven to 375° F.

2 Combine soy milk and lemon juice, and let sit for 10 minutes until it curdles (this is a good thing!).

3 Sift together dry ingredients.

4 Stir in melted margarine, curdled soy milk, and raisins. Dough will be sticky.

5 Knead dough 10 times, and shape into a slightly flattened ball.

6 Place ball onto an ungreased cookie sheet, cut a cross on the top, and bake for 45 minutes.

7 Around minute 43, heat water and sugar together for glaze. Take bread out of the oven and pour glaze over top. Bake another 10 minutes.

Nutrition Snapshot

Per slice: 207 calories, 6 g total fat, 2 g saturated fat, 0 mg cholesterol, 345 mg sodium, 35 g carbohydrates, 1.5 g fiber, 11 g sugar, 4 g protein, 1% vitamin A, 1% vitamin C, 10.5% calcium, 8% iron

Note Using whole wheat flour will make the bread too dense. Enjoy all-purpose flour for a change, and load up on a few extra higher-fiber foods while you celebrate the Emerald Isle.

Makes 12 slices
Prep time 15 minutes
Hands-off cooking time 45 minutes plus another 10 minutes after adding glaze

Minty Fruit Salad

Refreshing fruit salad is a perfect finish to a hearty meal, or a delightful treat first thing in the morning alongside Breakfast Patties *(page 61). Mint helps with digestion and fresh breath. If need be, skip the coconut, and this recipe will still be righteous.*

2 cups frozen Mango Chunks, thawed, or 1 mango, cut into chunks

2 cups watermelon chunks

2 cups pineapple chunks

⅓ cup chopped fresh mint

½ cup orange juice

2 Tbsp unsweetened shredded coconut

¼ tsp almond extract

1 Place fruit and mint in a medium-sized mixing bowl.

2 In a separate small bowl whisk together orange juice, coconut, and almond extract. Pour over fruit and mint and toss gently.

3 Enjoy immediately, and store leftovers in the fridge for up to 1 day.

Nutrition Snapshot

Per serving: 85 calories, 1.5 g total fat, 1 g saturated fat, 0 mg cholesterol, 2 mg sodium, 18.5 g carbohydrates, 2 g fiber, 15.5 g sugar, 1 g protein, 9.5% vitamin A, 48.5% vitamin C, 1.5% calcium, 2% iron

G
Gluten Free

Makes 6 (1-cup) servings
Prep time 10 minutes

Hot Pants Cornbread

Cornbread pretty much lets you enjoy cake for dinner, and who could turn that down?
This recipe knocks out all the cholesterol by replacing the egg and milk with flaxseed meal
and unsweetened almond milk, and uses half the amount of oil recommended. Jalapeños are
added not only to heat things up, but to bring you down from your "cake for dinner" euphoria.
Enjoy this version as a starchy side dish to many meals, but most definitely the Chili Cook-Off
(page 188).

1 Tbsp flaxseed meal (ground flaxseeds), soaked in 3 Tbsp warm filtered water
for 10 minutes until it forms a gel, or 1 Tbsp cornstarch dissolved in 2 Tbsp warm water

¼ cup vegetable oil, such as grapeseed oil

¾ cup unsweetened almond milk, or other unsweetened non-dairy milk

1 (15-oz) box Cornbread Mix

2 jalapeño peppers, seeded and diced

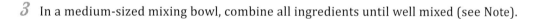

1 Preheat oven to 350° F.

2 Lightly grease a 9 x 9-inch baking dish.

3 In a medium-sized mixing bowl, combine all ingredients until well mixed (see Note).

4 Pour batter into baking dish and bake for 35-40 minutes until a toothpick inserted
in center comes out clean.

5 Enjoy immediately and store leftovers in a tightly closed container for 3 days, or in
the fridge for up to 5 days. Individual wrapped portions will keep in the freezer for
up to 2 months.

Nutrition Snapshot
*Per slice: 231 calories, 6.5 g total fat, 0.5 g saturated fat, 0 mg cholesterol, 255 mg sodium,
38.5 g carbohydrates, 1.5 g fiber, 15 g sugar, 3.5 g protein, 3.5% vitamin A, 2.5% vitamin C,
2% calcium, 6.5% iron*

Note Alternatively, combine all ingredients in mixing bowl except diced jalapeños, and
sprinkle those on top once the batter is poured into the baking pan. This method is a good way
to keep portions of the bread jalapeño-free.

Tip Make this recipe even healthier by adding a shredded carrot and/or a shredded zucchini.

Makes 9 slices
Prep time 10 minutes
Hands-off cooking time 35 minutes

Energy Bars

If you rely on pre-packaged energy bars for between-meal snacks, make up a batch or double batch of these to save moolah. They're cheap to make and quite scrumptious. Pepitas—Mexican pumpkin seeds—are high in protein, iron, zinc, and the eye-protecting compound lutein. For variation, use whichever nuts, seeds, or nut butter you like to satisfy your gourmet taste buds. Alternatively, leave out the sunflower seed butter and bake this in a 9 x 13-inch pan for 30 minutes to make a tasty granola.

1 Tbsp flaxseed meal (ground flaxseeds), soaked in 3 Tbsp warm filtered water for 10 minutes until it forms a gel, or 1 Tbsp cornstarch dissolved in 2 Tbsp warm water

1 cup old-fashioned rolled oats

½ cup unsweetened shredded coconut (optional)

1 cup Roasted and Salted Pepitas, or other seeds or crushed nuts

¼ cup packed raisins

1 ripe banana

½ cup sunflower seed butter, peanut butter, or other seed or nut butter

¼ cup agave nectar

1 tsp vanilla

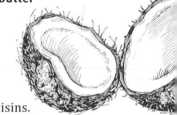

1   Preheat oven to 350° F.

2   In a large mixing bowl, combine oats, coconut (if using), pepitas, and raisins.

3   In a separate small microwave-safe bowl, microwave sunflower seed butter, agave, and vanilla for 30 seconds. Stir together until well-mixed. Add ripe banana and crush with a fork to combine. Stir in gelatinized flaxseed meal mixture.

4   Press firmly into a lightly greased 9 x 9-inch baking dish, and bake for 15 minutes. Chill in the fridge for 45 minutes before slicing.

5   Store leftovers in the fridge for up to 5 days, or in individually wrapped bags in the freezer for up to 2 months.

Nutrition Snapshot

Per bar: 184 calories, 10 g total fat, 1.5 g saturated fat, 0 mg cholesterol, 94 mg sodium, 18.5 g carbohydrates, 3 g fiber, 10 g sugar, 6.5 g protein, 1% vitamin A, 1.5% vitamin C, 1.5% calcium, 13.5% iron

Makes   12 bars
Prep time   5 minutes
Hands-off cooking time   15 minutes
plus 45 minutes to chill

Extras

Perfect Brown Rice

Brown rice is wonderfully nutty, and while it takes a bit longer to cook than white rice, the fancy method of toasting it described below cuts down on the cooking time by about 5 minutes. Brown rice is loaded with B vitamins and fiber and comes in a variety of types. The long-grain varieties are light and fluffy, while the short-grain types are denser and chewier. Basmati and jasmine varieties are especially fragrant and flavorful. When you make brown rice, make a lot and freeze ¾-cup-size portions for up to 3 months. Thaw for quick dinner prep later on.

3 cups Brown Basmati Rice, or other brown rice variety
6 cups filtered water

1 Heat brown rice in a dry, large cooking pot over medium-high heat until rice starts to crackle, about 3 minutes. Continue to toast, stirring for about 3 more minutes.

2 Add cooking water, bring to a boil, and then reduce heat to simmer for 35 minutes, or until all water is absorbed.

Nutrition Snapshot
Per ¾ cup: 160 calories, 1.5 g total fat, 0 g saturated fat, 0 mg cholesterol, 0 mg sodium, 35 g carbohydrates, 1 g fiber, 0 g sugar, 3 g protein, 0% vitamin A, 0% vitamin C, 0% calcium, 4% iron

Tip To get a perfect ratio of rice to water, place any amount of rice in your cooking pot and make sure it's level. Add water enough so that when the tip of your finger touches the top of the rice, the water meets the first notch or bend in your finger. No matter what size your finger, this trick makes perfect rice every time! I learned this from a friend in the Maldives.

Makes 12 (¾-cup) servings (9 cups total)
Prep time 10 minutes
Hands–off cooking time 35 minutes

Tofu Mayo

Even low-calorie and olive oil mayos have saturated fat, cholesterol, and too many calories. This version is like the goody-goody twin sister—it looks and tastes the same, but it's egg-free, cholesterol-free, and actually good for you!

½ (16-oz) block Organic Firm Tofu
2 Tbsp brown rice vinegar
2 Tbsp grapeseed oil
½ tsp salt
Dash black pepper (one shake)

1 In a blender or food processor, blend all ingredients until creamy.

2 Store mayo in an airtight container in the fridge for up to 10 days.

Nutrition Snapshot
Per Tbsp: 19 calories, 1.5 g total fat, 0 g saturated fat, 0 mg cholesterol, 50 mg sodium, 0 g carbohydrates, 0 g fiber, 0 g sugar, 1 g protein, 0% vitamin A, 0% vitamin C, 1% calcium, 1% iron

Makes about 1 ½ cups (24 Tablespoons)
Prep time 5 minutes

Tahini Dressing for Veggies

This dressing is so easy, so good, so easy, and so good! It will get you eating more veggies in no time. Use it for dipping raw or steamed veggies, thinned with 2 more tablespoons water for salad dressing, or even as a falafel or Hot Chickpea Burger *(page 153) condiment. Tahini is made from sesame seeds which are a great source of calcium and iron.*

1/3 **cup tahini (sesame seed butter)**
1/3 **cup water**
1/4 **cup lemon juice**
2 cloves garlic, 2 tsp garlic powder , or 2 cubes frozen Crushed Garlic
3/4 **tsp salt**

1 Blend ingredients together until smooth. Add additional water, 1 Tbsp at a time, for a thinner dressing.

2 Store dressing in the fridge for up to 5 days. Stir or re-blend if dressing separates.

Nutrition Snapshot
Per Tbsp: 35 calories, 3 g total fat, 0.5 g saturated fat, 0 mg cholesterol, 116 mg sodium, 1.5 g carbohydrates, 0.5 g fiber, 0 g sugar, 1 g protein, 0% vitamin A, 3% vitamin C, 2.5% calcium, 3% iron

Note Alternatively, use unsalted almond butter in place of tahini for an equally delicious dressing.

G
Gluten Free

Makes 1 cup (16 Tablespoons)
Prep time 3 minutes

Simple Salad Dressing

This zippy dressing will excite lettuce like no other bottled version around. "You made your own dressing?" You sure did. In less than 3 minutes!

½ cup olive oil
1 Tbsp spicy brown mustard
¼ cup white balsamic vinegar
½ tsp salt

1 In a tightly sealed container, place all ingredients and shake until mixed.

2 Store dressing in the fridge for up to 10 days. Re-mix if dressing separates.

Nutrition Snapshot
Per Tbsp: 75 calories, 8.5 g total fat, 1 g saturated fat, 0 mg cholesterol, 103 mg sodium, 1 g carbohydrates, 0 g fiber, 1 g sugar, 0 g protein, 0% vitamin A, 0% vitamin C, 0% calcium, 0% iron

G Gluten Free

Makes about ¾ cup (13 Tablespoons)
Prep time 2 minutes

Acknowledgments

Thank you:

Team Reilly (Brian, Keller, Griffin, and Jake) for your unedited feedback on recipes and patience as I boxed you out of my laboratory, was distracted with recipe creations during the most important meal conversations, and made you wait for dinner while I got the perfect photo shot.

Recipe contributors Kristin Doyle, RN, CNC, Sara Duke, Jan Graves, Gloria Huerta, Ami Karnosh, MS, CN, Angela Liddon, MA, Janet McKee, HHC, AADP, Rafael Prieto, Sandi Rechenmacher, Keller Reilly, Michael Reilly, and Christine Sproat, OT—without you, this book would have much less pizzazz.

Kris Carr for your daily affirmations, green juice and smoothie prescriptions, countless and addictive rays of sunshine, and igniting this book with your sparkly foreword.

Stefan Lopatkiewicz, Esq., my legal advisor, agent, part-time taste-tester, and dear family friend. Without you, I'd still be wondering whether or not I should write a hardback book in an e-book world, and how to make a great martini.

Nigel Purvis, and Alison and Pete Duvall of Anything Photographic for getting me from 0-60 in photography overnight, including cameras, lenses, and gear. Cheese!

Eric Cawthon, PA, and Harrison Solomon, MD who stitched, treated, and repaired my left index finger after I blended it in my immersion blender while creating the Squash Drop Cookies. The dangerous blending step has been omitted from the final version of the recipe.

Charlotte Keller, my best friend and mom, who infused me with wheat germ, sesame peanut butter from Walnut Acres, and something raw at every one of my childhood meals. This is no doubt to blame for catapulting me into vegetable preachery and my current role as a health disciple.

Arnold Keller, the smartest person I know and dad, who designed and built the most bitchin' gourmet kitchen for the skinniest of recipe creations. Without all the extra counter space and turbo oven hood, I never could have made 100 recipes with such ease.

Linda Reilly, the best mom-in-law and dishwasher on the East coast. Without you, I'd still be buried in dirty dishes and trying to find the kids.

Eric Hutchinson, Christopher Keller, Mumford & Sons, and The Avett Brothers for providing energizing and recipe-inspiring background music.

Lisa Büttner who loaned me dishes, napkins, placemats, and many of the other non-food photo props to make the pix much snazzier. And I didn't break a single thing!

Lilla Hangay, my superhuman graphic designer who splashed this book with color, character, and charm, and is the real reason you can't wait to see the next page.

Heather World, my genius copy editor who not only smoothed out all the bumps, but also let a few essential run-ons and fragments slip through the cracks to maintain the fun nature of healthy eating.

Deana Gunn and Wona Miniati, a dynamic tour de force who found me, believed in me, and taught me everything I know about constructing an exceptional book.

And last but not least, Trader Joe's, for not only making grocery shopping a happy affair and a fun-filled field trip for the kids (no matter how full my cart), but for also inspiring heaps of simple, healthy, and scrumptious recipes. See you tomorrow!

Recipe Index

No-Gluten Recipe Index

Recipes that are No-Gluten or can easily be made No-Gluten (*) using simple substitutions

⑦ Store Locations

Arizona

Ahwatukee # 177
4025 E. Chandler Blvd.,
Ste. 38
Ahwatukee, AZ 85048
Phone: 480-759-2295

Glendale # 085
7720 West Bell Road
Glendale, AZ 85308
Phone: 623-776-7414

Mesa # 089
2050 East Baseline Rd.
Mesa, AZ 85204
Phone: 480-632-0951

Paradise Valley # 282
4726 E. Shea Blvd.
Phoenix, AZ 85028
Phone: 602-485-7788

**Phoenix
(Town & Country) # 090**
4821 N. 20th Street
Phoenix, AZ 85016
Phone: 602-912-9022

Scottsdale (North) # 087
7555 E. Frank Lloyd Wright
N. Scottsdale, AZ 85260
Phone: 480-367-8920

Scottsdale # 094
6202 N. Scottsdale Road
Scottsdale, AZ 85253
Phone: 480-948-9886

Surprise # 092
14095 West Grand Ave.
Surprise, AZ 85374
Phone: 623-546-1640

Tempe # 093
6460 S. McClintock Drive
Tempe, AZ 85283
Phone: 480-838-4142

**Tucson
(Crossroads) # 088**
4766 East Grant Road
Tucson, AZ 85712
Phone: 520-323-4500

**Tucson (Wilmot &
Speedway)# 095**
1101 N. Wilmot Rd.
Suite #147
Tucson, AZ 85712
Phone: 520-733-1313

**Tucson (Campbell &
Limberlost) # 191**
4209 N. Campbell Ave.
Tucson, AZ 85719
Phone: 520-325-0069

Tucson - Oro Valley # 096
7912 N. Oracle
Oro Valley, AZ 85704
Phone: 520-797-4207

California

Agoura Hills
28941 Canwood Street
Agoura Hills, CA 91301
Phone: 818-865-8217

Alameda # 109
2217 South Shore Center
Alameda, CA 94501
Phone: 510-769-5450

Aliso Viejo # 195
The Commons
26541 Aliso Creek Road
Aliso Viejo, CA 92656
Phone: 949-643-5531

Arroyo Grande # 117
955 Rancho Parkway
Arroyo Grande, CA 93420
Phone: 805-474-6114

Bakersfield # 014
8200-C 21 Stockdale Hwy.
Bakersfield, CA 93311
Phone: 661-837-8863

Berkeley #186
1885 University Ave.
Berkeley, CA 94703
Phone: 510-204-9074

Bixby Knolls # 116
4121 Atlantic Ave.
Bixby Knolls, CA 90807
Phone: 562-988-0695

Brea # 011
2500 E. Imperial Hwy.
Suite 177
Brea, CA 92821
Phone 714-257-1180

Brentwood # 201
5451 Lone Tree Way
Brentwood, CA 94513
Phone: 925-516-3044

Burbank # 124
214 East Alameda
Burbank, CA 91502
Phone: 818-848-4299

Camarillo # 114
363 Carmen Drive
Camarillo, CA 93010
Phone: 805-388-1925

Campbell # 073
1875 Bascom Avenue
Campbell, CA 95008
Phone: 408-369-7823

Capitola # 064
3555 Clares Street #D
Capitola, CA 95010
Phone: 831-464-0115

Carlsbad # 220
2629 Gateway Road
Carlsbad, CA 92009
Phone: 760-603-8473

Castro Valley # 084
22224 Redwood Road
Castro Valley, CA 94546
Phone: 510-538-2738

Cathedral City # 118
67-720 East Palm Cyn.
Cathedral City, CA 92234
Phone: 760-202-0090

Cerritos # 104
12861 Towne Center Drive
Cerritos, CA 90703
Phone: 562-402-5148

Chatsworth # 184
10330 Mason Ave.
Chatsworth, CA 91311
Phone: 818-341-3010

Chico # 199
801 East Ave., Suite #110
Chico, CA 95926
Phone: 530-343-9920

Chino Hills # 216
13911 Peyton Dr.
Chino Hills, CA 91709
Phone: 909-627-1404

Chula Vista # 120
878 Eastlake Parkway,
Suite 810
Chula Vista, CA 91914
Phone: 619-656-5370

Claremont # 214
475 W. Foothill Blvd.
Claremont, CA 91711
Phone: 909-625-8784

Clovis # 180
1077 N. Willow, Suite 101
Clovis, CA 93611
Phone: 559-325-3120

**Concord (Oak Grove
& Treat) # 083**
785 Oak Grove Road
Concord, CA 94518
Phone: 925-521-1134

Concord (Airport) # 060
1150 Concord Ave.
Concord, CA 94520
Phone: 925-689-2990

Corona # 213
2790 Cabot Drive, Ste. 165
Corona, CA 92883
Phone: 951-603-0299

Costa Mesa # 035
640 W. 17th Street
Costa Mesa, CA 92627
Phone: 949-642-5134

Culver City # 036
9290 Culver Blvd.
Culver City, CA 90232
Phone: 310-202-1108

Daly City # 074
417 Westlake Center
Daly City, CA 94015
Phone: 650-755-3825

Danville # 065
85 Railroad Ave.
Danville, CA 94526
Phone: 925-838-5757

Davis
885 Russell Blvd.
Davis, CA 95616
Phone: 530-757-2693

Eagle Rock # 055
1566 Colorado Blvd.
Eagle Rock, CA 90041
Phone: 323-257-6422

El Cerrito # 108
225 El Cerrito Plaza
El Cerrito, CA 94530
Phone: 510-524-7609

Elk Grove # 190
9670 Bruceville Road
Elk Grove, CA 95757
Phone: 916-686-9980

Emeryville # 072
5700 Christie Avenue
Emeryville, CA 94608
Phone: 510-658-8091

Encinitas # 025
115 N. El Camino Real,
Suite A
Encinitas, CA 92024
Phone: 760-634-2114

Encino # 056
17640 Burbank Blvd.
Encino, CA 91316
Phone: 818-990-7751

Escondido # 105
1885 So. Centre City
Pkwy., Unit "A"
Escondido, CA 92025
Phone: 760-233-4020

Fair Oaks # 071
5309 Sunrise Blvd.
Fair Oaks, CA 95628
Phone: 916-863-1744

Fairfield # 101
1350 Gateway Blvd.,
Suite A1-A7
Fairfield, CA 94533
Phone: 707-434-0144

Folsom # 172
850 East Bidwell
Folsom, CA 95630
Phone: 916-817-8820

Fremont # 077
39324 Argonaut Way
Fremont, CA 94538
Phone: 510-794-1386

Fresno # 008
5376 N. Blackstone
Fresno, CA 93710
Phone: 559-222-4348

Glendale # 053
130 N. Glendale Ave.
Glendale, CA 91206
Phone: 818-637-2990

Goleta # 110
5767 Calle Real
Goleta, CA 93117
Phone: 805-692-2234

Granada Hills # 044
11114 Balboa Blvd.
Granada Hills, CA 91344
Phone: 818-368-6461

Hollywood
1600 N. Vine Street
Los Angeles, CA 90028
Phone: 323-856-0689

Huntington Bch. # 047
18681-101 Main Street
Huntington Bch., CA 92648
Phone: 714-848-9640

Huntington Bch. # 241
21431 Brookhurst St.
Huntington Bch., CA 92646
Phone: 714-968-4070

Huntington Harbor # 244
Huntington Harbour Mall
16821 Algonquin St.
Huntington Bch., CA 92649
Phone: 714-846-7307

**Irvine (Walnut Village
Center) # 037**
14443 Culver Drive
Irvine, CA 92604
Phone: 949-857-8108

**Irvine (University
Center) # 111**
4225 Campus Dr.
Irvine, CA 92612
Phone: 949-509-6138

**Irvine (Irvine &
Sand Cyn) # 210**
6222 Irvine Blvd.
Irvine, CA 92620
Phone: 949-551-6402

La Cañada # 042
475 Foothill Blvd.
La Canada, CA 91011
Phone: 818-790-6373

La Crescenta # 052
3433 Foothill Blvd.
LaCrescenta, CA 91214
Phone: 818-249-3693

La Quinta # 189
46-400 Washington Street
La Quinta, CA 92253
Phone: 760-777-1553

Lafayette # 115
3649 Mt. Diablo Blvd.
Lafayette, CA 94549
Phone: 925-299-9344

Laguna Hills # 039
24321 Avenue De La Carlota
Laguna Hills, CA 92653
Phone: 949-586-8453

Laguna Niguel # 103
32351 Street of the Golden
Lantern
Laguna Niguel, CA 92677
Phone: 949-493-8599

La Jolla # 020
8657 Villa LaJolla
Drive #210
La Jolla, CA 92037
Phone: 858-546-8629

La Mesa # 024
5495 Grossmont Center Dr.
La Mesa, CA 91942
Phone: 619-466-0105

Larkspur # 235
2052 Redwood Hwy
Larkspur, CA 94921
Phone: 415-945-7955

Livermore # 208
1122-A East Stanley Blvd.
Livermore, CA 94550
Phone: 925-243-1947

Long Beach (PCH) # 043
6451 E. Pacific Coast Hwy.
Long Beach, CA 90803
Phone: 562-596-4388

**Long Beach
(Bellflower Blvd.) # 194**
2222 Bellflower Blvd.
Long Beach, CA 90815
Phone: 562-596-2514

Los Altos # 127
2310 Homestead Rd.
Los Altos, CA 94024
Phone: 408-245-1917

**Los Angeles
(Silver Lake) # 017**
2738 Hyperion Ave.
Los Angeles, CA 90027
Phone: 323-665-6774

Los Angeles # 031
263 S. La Brea
Los Angeles, CA 90036
Phone: 323-965-1989

**Los Angeles
(Sunset Strip) # 192**
8000 Sunset Blvd.
Los Angeles, CA 90046
Phone: 323-822-7663

Los Gatos # 181
15466 Los Gatos Blvd.
Los Gatos, CA 95032
Phone 408-356-2324

Manhattan Beach # 034
1821 Manhattan
Beach. Blvd.
Manhattan Bch., CA 90266
Phone: 310-372-1274

Manhattan Beach # 196
1800 Rosecrans Blvd.
Manhattan Beach,
CA 90266
Phone: 310-725-9800

Menlo Park # 069
720 Menlo Avenue
Menlo Park, CA 94025
Phone: 650-323-2134

Millbrae # 170
765 Broadway
Millbrae, CA 94030
Phone: 650-259-9142

Mission Viejo # 126
25410 Marguerite Parkway
Mission Viejo, CA 92692
Phone: 949-581-5638

Modesto # 009
3250 Dale Road
Modesto, CA 95356
Phone: 209-491-0445

Monrovia # 112
604 W. Huntington Dr.
Monrovia, CA 91016
Phone: 626-358-8884

Monterey # 204
570 Munras Ave., Ste. 20
Monterey, CA 93940
Phone: 831-372-2010

Morgan Hill # 202
17035 Laurel Road
Morgan Hill, CA 95037
Phone: 408-778-6409

Mountain View # 081
590 Showers Dr.
Mountain View, CA 94040
Phone: 650-917-1013

Napa # 128
3654 Bel Aire Plaza
Napa, CA 94558
Phone: 707-256-0806

Newbury Park # 243
125 N. Reino Road
Newbury Park, CA
Phone: 805-375-1984

Newport Beach # 125
8086 East Coast Highway
Newport Beach, CA 92657
Phone: 949-494-7404

Novato # 198
7514 Redwood Blvd.
Novato, CA 94945
Phone: 415-898-9359

**Oakland
(Lakeshore) # 203**
3250 Lakeshore Ave.
Oakland, CA 94610
Phone: 510-238-9076

**Oakland
(Rockridge) # 231**
5727 College Ave.
Oakland, CA 94618
Phone: 510-923-9428

Oceanside # 22
2570 Vista Way
Oceanside, CA 92054
Phone: 760-433-9994

Orange # 046
2114 N. Tustin St.
Orange, CA 92865
Phone: 714-283-5697

Pacific Grove # 008
1170 Forest Avenue
Pacific Grove, CA 93950
Phone: 831-656-0180

Palm Desert # 003
44-250 Town Center Way,
Suite C6
Palm Desert, CA 92260
Phone: 760-340-2291

Palmdale # 185
39507 10th Street West
Palmdale, CA 93551
Phone: 661-947-2890

Palo Alto # 207
855 El Camino Real
Palo Alto, CA 94301
Phone: 650-327-7018

**Pasadena
(S. Lake Ave.) # 179**
345 South Lake Ave.
Pasadena, CA 91101
Phone: 626-395-9553

**Pasadena
(S. Arroyo Pkwy.) # 051**
610 S. Arroyo Parkway
Pasadena, CA 91105
Phone: 626-568-9254

**Pasadena
(Hastings Ranch) # 171**
467 Rosemead Blvd.
Pasadena, CA 91107
Phone: 626-351-3399

Petaluma # 107
169 North McDowell Blvd.
Petaluma, CA 94954
Phone: 707-769-2782

Pinole # 230
2742 Pinole Valley Rd.
Pinole, CA 94564
Phone: 510-222-3501

Pleasanton # 066
4040 Pimlico #150
Pleasanton, CA 94588
Phone: 925-225-3600

Rancho Cucamonga # 217
6401 Haven Ave.
Rancho Cucamonga, CA
91737
Phone: 909-476-1410

**Rancho Palos Verdes
057**
28901 S. Western Ave. #243
Rancho Palos Verdes,
CA 90275
Phone: 310-832-1241

Rancho Palos Verdes # 233
31176 Hawthorne Blvd.
Rancho Palos Verdes,
CA 90275
Phone: 310-544-1727

**Rancho Santa
Margarita # 027**
30652 Santa Margarita
Pkwy. Suite F102
Rancho Santa Margarita, CA
92688
Phone: 949-888-3640

Redding # 219
845 Browning St.
Redding, CA 96003
Phone: 530-223-4875

Redlands # 099
552 Orange Street Plaza
Redlands, CA 92374
Phone: 909-798-3888

Redondo Beach # 038
1761 S. Elena Avenue
Redondo Bch., CA 90277
Phone: 310-316-1745

Riverside # 15
6225 Riverside Plaza
Riverside, CA 92506
Phone: 951-682-4684

Roseville # 80
1117 Roseville Square
Roseville, CA 95678
Phone: 916-784-9084

**Sacramento
(Folsom Blvd.) # 175**
5000 Folsom Blvd.
Sacramento, CA 95819
Phone: 916-456-1853

**Sacramento
(Fulton & Marconi) # 070**
2625 Marconi Avenue
Sacramento, CA 95821
Phone: 916-481-8797

San Carlos # 174
1482 El Camino Real
San Carlos, CA 94070
Phone: 650-594-2138

San Clemente # 016
638 Camino DeLosMares,
Sp.#115-G
San Clemente, CA 92673
Phone: 949-240-9996

**San Diego
(Hillcrest) # 026**
1090 University Ste.
G100-107
San Diego, CA 92103
Phone: 619-296-3122

**San Diego
(Point Loma) # 188**
2401 Truxtun Rd., Ste. 300
San Diego, CA 92106
Phone: 619-758-9272

**San Diego
(Pacific Beach) # 021**
1211 Garnet Avenue
San Diego, CA 92109
Phone: 858-272-7235

**San Diego (Carmel
Mtn. Ranch) # 023**
11955 Carmel Mtn. Rd.
#702
San Diego, CA 92128
Phone: 858-673-0526

**San Diego
(Scripps Ranch) # 221**
9850 Hibert Street
San Diego, CA 92131
Phone: 858-549-9185

San Dimas # 028
856 Arrow Hwy. "C"
Target Center
San Dimas, CA 91773
Phone: 909-305-4757

**San Francisco
(9th Street) # 078**
555 9th Street
San Francisco, CA 94103
Phone: 415-863-1292

**San Francisco
(Masonic Ave.) # 100**
3 Masonic Avenue
San Francisco, CA 94118
Phone: 415-346-9964

**San Francisco
(North Beach) # 019**
401 Bay Street
San Francisco, CA 94133
Phone: 415-351-1013

**San Francisco
(Stonestown) # 236**
265 Winston Dr.
San Francisco, CA 94132
Phone: 415-665-1835

San Gabriel # 032
7260 N. Rosemead Blvd.
San Gabriel, CA 91775
Phone: 626-285-5862

San Jose (Bollinger) # 232
7250 Bollinger Rd.
San Jose, CA 95129
Phone: 408-873-7384

San Jose (Coleman Ave) # 212
635 Coleman Ave.
San Jose, CA 95110
Phone: 408-298-9731

San Jose (Old Almaden) # 063
5353 Almaden Expressway #J-38
San Jose, CA 95118
Phone: 408-927-9091

San Jose (Westgate West) # 062
5269 Prospect
San Jose, CA 95129
Phone: 408-446-5055

San Luis Obispo # 041
3977 Higuera Street
San Luis Obispo, CA 93401
Phone: 805-783-2780

San Mateo (Grant Street) # 067
1820-22 S. Grant Street
San Mateo, CA 94402
Phone: 650-570-6140

San Mateo (Hillsdale) # 245
45 W Hillsdale Blvd
San Mateo, CA 94403
Phone: 650-286-1509

San Rafael # 061
337 Third Street
San Rafael, CA 94901
Phone: 415-454-9530

Santa Ana # 113
3329 South Bristol Street
Santa Ana, CA 92704
Phone: 714-424-9304

Santa Barbara (S. Milpas St.) # 059
29 S. Milpas Street
Santa Barbara, CA 93103
Phone: 805-564-7878

Santa Barbara (De La Vina) # 183
3025 De La Vina
Santa Barbara, CA 93105
Phone: 805-563-7383

Santa Cruz # 193
700 Front Street
Santa Cruz, CA 95060
Phone: 831-425-0140

Santa Maria # 239
1303 S. Bradley Road
Santa Maria, CA 93454
Phone: 805-925-1657

Santa Monica # 006
3212 Pico Blvd.
Santa Monica, CA 90405
Phone: 310-581-0253

Santa Rosa (Cleveland Ave.) # 075
3225 Cleveland Avenue
Santa Rosa, CA 95403
Phone: 707-525-1406

Santa Rosa (Santa Rosa Ave.) # 178
2100 Santa Rosa Ave.
Santa Rosa, CA 95407
Phone: 707-535-0788

Sherman Oaks # 049
14119 Riverside Drive
Sherman Oaks, CA 91423
Phone: 818-789-2771

Simi Valley # 030
2975-A Cochran St.
Simi Valley, CA 93065
Phone: 805-520-3135

South Pasadena # 018
613 Mission Street
South Pasadena, CA 91030
Phone: 626-441-6263

South San Francisco # 187
301 McLellan Dr.
So. San Francisco, CA 94080
Phone: 650-583-6401

Stockton # 076
6535 Pacific Avenue
Stockton, CA 95207
Phone: 209-951-7597

Studio City # 122
11976 Ventura Blvd.
Studio City, CA 91604
Phone: 818-509-0168

Sunnyvale # 068
727 Sunnyvale/
Saratoga Rd.
Sunnyvale, CA 94087
Phone: 408-481-9082

Temecula # 102
40665 Winchester Rd., Bldg. B, Ste. 4-6
Temecula, CA 92591
Phone: 951-296-9964

Templeton # 211
1111 Rossi Road
Templeton, CA 93465
Phone: 805-434-9562

Thousand Oaks # 196
451 Avenida
De Los Arboles
Thousand Oaks, CA 91360
Phone: 805-492-7107

Toluca Lake # 054
10130 Riverside Drive
Toluca Lake, CA 91602
Phone: 818-762-2787

Torrance (Hawthorne Blvd.) # 121
19720 Hawthorne Blvd.
Torrance, CA 90503
Phone: 310-793-8585

Torrance (Rolling Hills Plaza) # 029
2545 Pacific Coast Highway
Torrance, CA 90505
Phone: 310-326-9520

Tustin # 197
12932 Newport Avenue
Tustin, CA 92780
Phone: 714-669-3752

Upland # 010
333 So. Mountain Avenue
Upland, CA 91786
Phone: 909-946-4799

Valencia # 013
26517 Bouquet Canyon Rd
Santa Clarita, CA 91350
Phone: 661-263-3796

Ventura # 045
1795 S. Victoria Avenue
Ventura, CA 93003
Phone: 805-650-9977

Ventura – Midtown
103 S. Mills Road Suite 104
Ventura, CA 93003
Phone: 805-658-2664

Walnut Creek # 123
1372 So. California Blvd.
Walnut Creek, CA 94596
Phone: 925-945-1674

West Hills # 050
6751 Fallbrook Ave.
West Hills, CA 91307
Phone: 818-347-2591

West Hollywood # 040
7304 Santa Monica Blvd.
West Hollywood, CA 90046
Phone: 323-851-9772

West Hollywood # 173
8611 Santa Monica Blvd.
West Hollywood, CA 90069
Phone: 310-657-0152

West Los Angeles (National Blvd.) # 007
10850 National Blvd.
West Los Angeles, CA 90064
Phone: 310-470-1917

West Los Angeles S. Sepulveda Blvd.) # 119
3456 S. Sepulveda Blvd.
West Los Angeles, CA 90034
Phone: 310-836-2458

West Los Angeles (Olympic) # 215
11755 W. Olympic Blvd.
West Los Angeles, CA 90064
Phone: 310-477-5949

Westchester # 033
8645 S. Sepulveda
Westchester, CA 90045
Phone: 310-338-9238

Westlake Village # 058
3835 E. Thousand Oaks Blvd.
Westlake Village, CA 91362
Phone: 805-494-5040

Westwood # 234
1000 Glendon Avenue
Los Angeles, CA 90024
Phone: 310-824-1495

Whittier # 048
15025 E. Whittier Blvd.
Whittier, CA 90603
Phone: 562-698-1642

Woodland Hills # 209
21054 Clarendon St.
Woodland Hills, CA 91364
Phone: 818-712-9475

Yorba Linda # 176
19655 Yorba Linda Blvd.
Yorba Linda, CA 92886
Phone: 714-970-0116

Connecticut

Danbury # 525
113 Mill Plain Rd.
Danbury, CT 06811
Phone: 203-739-0098
Alcohol: Beer Only

Darien # 522
436 Boston Post Rd.
Darien, CT 06820
Phone: 203-656-1414
Alcohol: Beer Only

Fairfield # 523
2258 Black Rock Turnpike
Fairfield, CT 06825
Phone: 203-330-8301
Alcohol: Beer Only

Orange # 524
560 Boston Post Road
Orange, CT 06477
Phone: 203-795-5505
Alcohol: Beer Only

West Hartford # 526
1489 New Britain Ave.
West Hartford, CT 06110
Phone: 860-561-4771
Alcohol: Beer Only

Westport # 521
400 Post Road East
Westport, CT 06880
Phone: 203-226-8966
Alcohol: Beer Only

Delaware

Wilmington* # 536
5605 Concord Pike
Wilmington, DE 19803
Phone: 302-478-8494

District of Columbia

Washington # 653
1101 25th Street NW
Washington, DC 20037
Phone: 202-296-1921

Georgia

Athens
1850 Epps Bridge Parkway
Athens, GA 30606
Phone: 706-583-8934

Atlanta (Buckhead) # 735
3183 Peachtree Rd NE
Atlanta, GA 30305
Phone: 404-842-0907

Atlanta (Midtown) # 730
931 Monroe Dr., NE
Atlanta, GA 30308
Phone: 404-815-9210

Marietta # 732
4250 Roswell Road
Marietta, GA 30062
Phone: 678-560-3585

Norcross # 734
5185 Peachtree Parkway,
Bld. 1200
Norcross, GA 30092
Phone: 678-966-9236

Roswell # 733
635 W. Crossville Road
Roswell, GA 30075
Phone: 770-645-8505

Sandy Springs # 731
6277 Roswell Road NE
Sandy Springs, GA 30328
Phone: 404-236-2414

Illinois

Algonquin # 699
1800 South Randall Road
Algonquin, IL 60102
Phone: 847-854-4886

Arlington Heights # 687
17 W. Rand Road
Arlington Heights, IL 60004
Phone: 847-506-0752

Batavia # 689
1942 West Fabyan
Parkway #222
Batavia, IL 60510
Phone: 630-879-3234

Chicago River North) # 696
44 E. Ontario St.
Chicago, IL 60611
Phone: 312-951-6369

Chicago (Lincoln & Grace) # 688
3745 North Lincoln Avenue
Chicago, IL 60613
Phone: 773-248-4920

Chicago (Lincoln Park) # 691
1840 North Clybourn
Avenue #200
Chicago, IL 60614
Phone: 312-274-9733

Chicago (South Loop) – coming soon!
1147 S. Wabash Ave.
Chicago, IL 60605
Phone: TBD

Chicago (Lakeview) – coming soon!
667 W. Diversey Pkwy
Chicago, IL 60614
Phone: 773-935-7255

Downers Grove # 683
122 Ogden Ave.
Downers Grove, IL 60515
Phone: 630-241-1662

Glen Ellyn # 680
680 Roosevelt Rd.
Glen Ellyn, IL 60137
Phone: 630-858-5077

Glenview # 681
1407 Waukegan Road
Glenview, IL 60025
Phone: 847-657-7821

La Grange # 685
25 North La Grange Road
La Grange, IL 60525
Phone: 708-579-0838

Lake Zurich # 684
735 W. Route 22**
Lake Zurich, IL 60047
Phone: 847-550-7827
[**For accurate driving directions using
GPS, please use 735 W Main Street]

Naperville # 690
44 West Gartner Road
Naperville, IL 60540
Phone: 630-355-4389

Northbrook # 682
127 Skokie Blvd.
Northbrook, IL 60062
Phone: 847-498-9076

Oak Park # 697
483 N. Harlem Ave.
Oak Park, IL 60301
Phone: 708-386-1169

Orland Park # 686
14924 S. La Grange Road
Orland Park, IL 60462
Phone: 708-349-9021

Park Ridge # 698
190 North Northwest
Highway
Park Ridge, IL 60068
Phone: 847-292-1108

Indiana

Indianapolis (Castleton) # 671
5473 East 82nd Street
Indianapolis, IN 46250
Phone: 317-595-8950

Indianapolis (West 86th) # 670
2902 West 86th Street
Indianapolis, IN 46268
Phone: 317-337-1880

Iowa

West Des Moines
6305 Mills Civic Parkway
West Des Moines, IA 50266
Phone: 515-225-3820

Kansas

Leawood* #723
4201 W 119th Street
Leawood, KS 66209
Phone: 913-327-7209

Maine

Portland # 519
87 Marginal Way
Portland, ME 04101
Phone: 207-699-3799

Maryland

Annapolis* # 650
160 F Jennifer Road
Annapolis, MD 21401
Phone: 410-573-0505

Bethesda* # 645
6831 Wisconsin Avenue
Bethesda, MD 20815
Phone: 301-907-0982

Columbia* # 658
6610 Marie Curie Dr.
(Int. of 175 & 108)
Elkridge, MD 21075
Phone: 410-953-8139

Gaithersburg* # 648
18270 Contour Rd.
Gaithersburg, MD 20877
Phone: 301-947-5953

Pikesville* # 655
1809 Reisterstown Road,
Suite #121
Pikesville, MD 21208
Phone: 410-484-8373

Rockville* # 642
12268-H Rockville Pike
Rockville, MD 20852
Phone: 301-468-6656

Silver Spring* # 652
10741 Columbia Pike
Silver Spring, MD 20901
Phone: 301-681-1675

Towson* # 649
1 E. Joppa Rd.
Towson, MD 21286
Phone: 410-296-9851

Massachusetts

Acton* # 511
145 Great Road
Acton, MA 01720
Phone: 978-266-8908

Arlington* # 505
1427 Massachusetts Ave.
Arlington, MA 02476
Phone: 781-646-9138

Boston #510
899 Boylston Street
Boston, MA 02115
Phone: 617-262-6505

Brookline # 501
1317 Beacon Street
Brookline, MA 02446
Phone: 617-278-9997

Burlington* # 515
51 Middlesex Turnpike
Burlington, MA 01803
Phone: 781-273-2310

Cambridge
748 Memorial Drive
Cambridge, MA 02139
Phone: 617-491-8582

**Cambridge
(Fresh Pond)* # 517**
211 Alewife Brook Pkwy
Cambridge, MA 02138
Phone: 617-498-3201

Framingham # 503
659 Worcester Road
Framingham, MA 01701
Phone: 508-935-2931

Hadley* # 512
375 Russell Street
Hadley, MA 01035
Phone: 413-587-3260

Hanover* # 513
1775 Washington Street
Hanover, MA 02339
Phone: 781-826-5389

Hyannis* # 514
Christmas Tree Promenade
655 Route 132, Unit 4-A
Hyannis, MA 02601
Phone: 508-790-3008

Needham Hts* 504
958 Highland Avenue
Needham Hts, MA 02494
Phone: 781-449-6993

Peabody* # 516
300 Andover Street,
Suite 15
Peabody, MA 01960
Phone: 978-977-5316

Saugus* # 506
358 Broadway, Unit B
(Shops @ Saugus, Rte. 1)
Saugus, MA 01906
Phone: 781-231-0369

Shrewsbury* # 508
77 Boston Turnpike
Shrewsbury, MA 01545
Phone: 508-755-9560

Tyngsboro* # 507
440 Middlesex Road
Tyngsboro, MA 01879
Phone: 978-649-2726

West Newton* # 509
1121 Washington St.
West Newton, MA 02465
Phone: 617-244-1620

Michigan

Ann Arbor # 678
2398 East Stadium Blvd.
Ann Arbor, MI 48104
Phone: 734-975-2455

Farmington Hills # 675
31221 West 14 Mile Road
Farmington Hills, MI 48334
Phone: 248-737-4609

Grosse Pointe # 665
17028 Kercheval Ave.
Grosse Pointe, MI 48230
Phone: 313-640-7794

Northville # 667
20490 Haggerty Road
Northville, MI 48167
Phone: 734-464-3675

Rochester Hills # 668
3044 Walton Blvd.
Rochester Hills, MI 48309
Phone: 248-375-2190

Royal Oak # 674
27880 Woodward Ave.
Royal Oak, MI 48067
Phone: 248-582-9002

Minnesota

Maple Grove # 713
12105 Elm Creek Blvd. N.
Maple Grove, MN 55369
Phone: 763-315-1739

Minnetonka # 714
11220 Wayzata Blvd
Minnetonka, MN 55305
Phone: 952-417-9080

Rochester
1200 16th St. SW
Rochester, NY 55902
Phone: 952-417-9080

St. Louis Park # 710
4500 Excelsior Blvd.
St. Louis Park, MN 55416
Phone: 952-285-1053

St. Paul # 716
484 Lexington Parkway S.
St. Paul, MN 55116
Phone: 651-698-3119

Woodbury # 715
8960 Hudson Road
Woodbury, MN 55125
Phone: 651-735-0269

Missouri

Brentwood # 792
48 Brentwood
Promenade Court
Brentwood, MO 63144
Phone: 314-963-0253

Chesterfield # 693
1679 Clarkson Road
Chesterfield, MO 63017
Phone: 636-536-7846

Creve Coeur # 694
11505 Olive Blvd.
Creve Coeur, MO 63141
Phone: 314-569-0427

Des Peres # 695
13343 Manchester Rd.
Des Peres, MO 63131
Phone: 314-984-5051

Kansas City –
coming soon!
8600 Ward Parkway
Kansas City, MO 64114
Phone: TBD

Nebraska

Lincoln
3120 Pine Lake Road,
Suite R
Lincoln, NE 68516
Phone: 402-328-0120

Omaha # 714
10305 Pacific St.
Omaha, NE 68114
Phone: 402-391-3698

Nevada

Anthem # 280
10345 South Eastern Ave.
Henderson, NV 89052
Phone: 702-407-8673

Carson City # 281
3790 US Highway 395 S,
Suite 401
Carson City, NV 89705
Phone: 775-267-2486

Henderson # 097
2716 North Green Valley
Parkway
Henderson, NV 89014
Phone: 702-433-6773

**Las Vegas
(Decatur Blvd.) # 098**
2101 S. Decatur Blvd.,
Suite 25
Las Vegas, NV 89102
Phone: 702-367-0227

**Las Vegas
(Summerlin) # 086**
7575 West Washington,
Suite 117
Las Vegas, NV 89128
Phone: 702-242-8240

Reno # 082
5035 S. McCarran Blvd.
Reno, NV 89502
Phone: 775-826-1621

New Jersey

Edgewater* # 606
715 River Road
Edgewater, NJ 07020
Phone: 201-945-5932

Florham Park* # 604
186 Columbia Turnpike
Florham Park, NJ 07932
Phone: 973-514-1511

Marlton* # 631
300 P Route 73 South
Marlton, NJ 08053
Phone: 856-988-3323

Millburn* # 609
187 Millburn Ave.
Millburn, NJ 07041
Phone: 973-218-0912

Paramus* # 605
404 Rt. 17 North
Paramus, NJ 07652
Phone: 201-265-9624

Princeton # 607
3528 US 1
(Brunswick Pike)
Princeton, NJ 08540
Phone: 609-897-0581

Shrewsbury*
1031 Broad St.
Shrewsbury, NJ 07702
Phone: 732-389-2535

Wayne* # 632
1172 Hamburg Turnpike
Wayne, NJ 07470
Phone: 973-692-0050

Westfield # 601
155 Elm St.
Westfield, NJ 07090
Phone: 908-301-0910

Westwood* # 602
20 Irvington Street
Westwood, NJ 07675
Phone: 201-263-0134

New Mexico

Albuquerque # 166
8928 Holly Ave. NE
Albuquerque, NM 87122
Phone: 505-796-0311

**Albuquerque
(Uptown) # 167**
2200 Uptown Loop NE
Albuquerque, NM 87110
Phone: 505-883-3662

Santa Fe # 165
530 W. Cordova Road
Santa Fe, NM 87505
Phone: 505-995-8145

New York

Brooklyn # 558
130 Court St
Brooklyn, NY 11201
Phone: 718-246-8460
Alcohol: Beer Only

Commack # 551
5010 Jericho Turnpike
Commack, NY 11725
Phone: 631-493-9210
Alcohol: Beer Only

Hartsdale # 533
215 North Central Avenue
Hartsdale, NY 10530
Phone: 914-997-1960
Alcohol: Beer Only

Hewlett # 554
1280 West Broadway
Hewlett, NY 11557
Phone: 516-569-7191
Alcohol: Beer Only

Lake Grove # 556
137 Alexander Ave.
Lake Grove, NY 11755
Phone: 631-863-2477
Alcohol: Beer Only

Larchmont # 532
1260 Boston Post Road
Larchmont, NY 10538
Phone: 914-833-9110
Alcohol: Beer Only

Merrick # 553
1714 Merrick Road
Merrick, NY 11566
Phone: 516-771-1012
Alcohol: Beer Only

**New York
(72nd & Broadway) # 542**
2075 Broadway
New York, NY 10023
Phone: 212-799-0028
Alcohol: Beer Only

**New York
(Chelsea) # 543**
675 6th Ave
New York, NY 10010
Phone: 212-255-2106
Alcohol: Beer Only

**New York (Union Square
Grocery) # 540**
142 E. 14th St.
New York, NY 10003
Phone: 212-529-4612
Alcohol: Beer Only

**New York (Union Square
Wine) # 541**
138 E. 14th St.
New York, NY 10003
Phone: 212-529-6326
Alcohol: Wine Only

Oceanside # 552
3418 Long Beach Rd.
Oceanside, NY 11572
Phone: 516-536-9163
Alcohol: Beer Only

Plainview # 555
425 S. Oyster Bay Rd.
Plainview, NY 11803
Phone: 516-933-6900
Alcohol: Beer Only

Queens # 557
90-30 Metropolitan Ave.
Queens, NY 11374
Phone: 718-275-1791
Alcohol: Beer Only

Scarsdale # 531
727 White Plains Rd.
Scarsdale, NY 10583
Phone: 914-472-2988
Alcohol: Beer Only

*Staten Island
– coming soon!*
2385 Richmond Ave
Staten Island, NY 10314
Phone: TBD
Alcohol: Beer Only

North Carolina

Cary # 741
1393 Kildaire Farms Rd.
Cary, NC 27511
Phone: 919-465-5984

Chapel Hill # 745
1800 E. Franklin St.
Chapel Hill, NC 27514
Phone: 919-918-7871

**Charlotte
(Midtown) # 744**
1133 Metropolitan Ave.,
Ste. 100
Charlotte, NC 28204
Phone: 704-334-0737

Charlotte (North) # 743
1820 East Arbors Dr.**
(corner of W. Mallard Creek
Church Rd. & Senator
Royall Dr.)
Charlotte, NC 28262
Phone: 704-688-9578
[**For accurate driving di-
rections on the web, please
use 1820 W. Mallard Creek
Church Rd.]

Charlotte (South) # 742
6418 Rea Rd.
Charlotte, NC 28277
Phone: 704-543-5249

Raleigh # 746
3000 Wake Forest Rd.
Raleigh, NC 27609
Phone: 919-981-7422

Ohio

Cincinnati # 669
7788 Montgomery Road
Cincinnati, OH 45236
Phone: 513-984-3452

Columbus # 679
3888 Townsfair Way
Columbus, OH 43219
Phone: 614-473-0794

Dublin # 672
6355 Sawmill Road
Dublin, OH 43017
Phone: 614-793-8505

Kettering # 673
328 East Stroop Road
Kettering, OH 45429
Phone: 937-294-5411

Westlake # 677
175 Market Street
Westlake, OH 44145
Phone: 440-250-1592

Woodmere # 676
28809 Chagrin Blvd.
Woodmere, OH 44122
Phone: 216-360-9320

Oregon

Beaverton # 141
11753 S. W. Beaverton
Hillsdale Hwy.
Beaverton, OR 97005
Phone: 503-626-3794

Bend # 150
63455 North
Highway 97, Ste. 4
Bend, OR 97701
Phone: 541-312-4198

Clackamas # 152
9345 SE 82nd Ave (across
from Home Depot)
Happy Valley, OR 97086
Phone: 503-771-6300

Corvallis # 154
1550 NW 9th Street
Corvallis, OR 97330
Phone: 541-753-0048

Eugene # 145
85 Oakway Center
Eugene, OR 97401
Phone: 541-485-1744

Hillsboro # 149
2285 NW 185th Ave.
Hillsboro, OR 97124
Phone: 503-645-8321

Lake Oswego # 142
15391 S. W. Bangy Rd.
Lake Oswego, OR 97035
Phone: 503-639-3238

Portland (SE) # 143
4715 S. E. 39th Avenue
Portland, OR 97202
Phone: 503-777-1601

Portland (NW) # 146
2122 N.W. Glisan
Portland, OR 97210
Phone: 971-544-0788

**Portland
(Hollywood) # 144**
4121 N.E. Halsey St.
Portland, OR 97213
Phone: 503-284-1694

Salem #153
4450 Commercial St.,
Suite 100
Salem, OR 97302
Phone: 503-378-9042

Pennsylvania

Ardmore* # 635
112 Coulter Avenue
Ardmore, PA 19003
Phone: 610-658-0645

Jenkintown* # 633
933 Old York Road
Jenkintown, PA 19046
Phone: 215-885-524

Media* # 637
12 East State Street
Media, PA 19063
Phone: 610-891-2752

North Wales* # 639
1430 Bethlehem Pike
(corner SR 309 & SR 63)
North Wales, PA 19454
Phone: 215-646-5870

Philadelphia* # 634
2121 Market Street
Philadelphia, PA 19103
Phone: 215-569-9282

Pittsburgh* # 638
6343 Penn Ave.
Pittsburgh, PA 15206
Phone: 412-363-5748

Pittsburgh
- coming soon!
1600 Washington Road
Pittsburgh, PA 15228
Phone: TBD

Wayne* # 632
171 East Swedesford Rd.
Wayne, PA 19087
Phone: 610-225-0925

Rhode Island

Warwick* # 518
1000 Bald Hill Rd
Warwick, RI 02886
Phone: 401-821-5368

South Carolina

Greenville
59 Woodruff
Industrial Lane
Greenville, SC 29607
Phone: 864-286-0231

Mt. Pleasant – #752
401 Johnnie Dodds Blvd.
Mt. Pleasant, SC 29464
Phone: 843-884-4037

Tennessee

Nashville # 664
3909 Hillsboro Pike
Nashville, TN 37215
Phone: 615-297-6560
Alcohol: Beer Only

Virginia

Alexandria # 647
612 N. Saint Asaph Street
Alexandria, VA 22314
Phone: 703-548-0611

Bailey's Crossroads # 644
5847 Leesburg Pike
Bailey's Crossroads,
VA 22041
Phone: 703-379-5883

Centreville # 654
14100 Lee Highway
Centreville, VA 20120
Phone: 703-815-0697

Fairfax # 643
9464 Main Street
Fairfax, VA 22031
Phone: 703-764-8550

Falls Church # 641
7514 Leesburg Turnpike
Falls Church, VA 22043
Phone: 703-288-0566

Newport News # 656
12551 Jefferson Ave.,
Suite #179
Newport News, VA 23602
Phone: 757-890-0235

Reston # 646
11958 Killingsworth Ave.
Reston, VA 20194
Phone: 703-689-0865

**Richmond
(Short Pump) # 659**
11331 W Broad St, Ste 161
Glen Allen, VA 23060
Phone: 804-360-4098

Springfield # 651
6394 Springfield Plaza
Springfield, VA 22150
Phone: 703-569-9301

Virginia Beach # 660
503 Hilltop Plaza
Virginia Beach, VA 23454
Phone: 757-422-4840

Williamsburg # 657
5000 Settlers Market Blvd
(corner of Monticello and
Settlers Market)**
Williamsburg, VA 23188
Phone: 757-259-2135
[**For accurate driving
directions on the web, please
use 5224 Monticello Ave.]

Washington

Ballard # 147
4609 14th Avenue NW
Seattle, WA 98107
Phone: 206-783-0498

Bellevue # 131
15400 N. E. 20th Street
Bellevue, WA 98007
Phone: 425-643-6885

Bellingham # 151
2410 James Street
Bellingham, WA 98225
Phone: 360-734-5166

Burien # 133
15868 1st. Avenue South
Burien, WA 98148
Phone: 206-901-9339

Everett # 139
811 S.E. Everett Mall Way
Everett, WA 98208
Phone: 425-513-2210

Federal Way # 134
1758 S. 320th Street
Federal Way, WA 98003
Phone: 253-529-9242

Issaquah # 138
1495 11th Ave. N.W.
Issaquah, WA 98027
Phone: 425-837-8088

Kirkland # 132
12632 120th Avenue N. E.
Kirkland, WA 98034
Phone: 425-823-1685

Lynnwood # 129
19500 Highway 99,
Suite 100
Lynnwood, WA 98036
Phone: 425-744-1346

Olympia # 156
Olympia West Center
1530 Black Lake Blvd.
Olympia, WA 98502
Phone: 360-352-7440

Redmond # 140
15932 Redmond Way
Redmond, WA 98052
Phone: 425-883-1624

Seattle (U. District) # 137
4555 Roosevelt Way NE
Seattle, WA 98105
Phone: 206-547-6299

**Seattle
(Queen Anne Hill) # 135**
112 West Galer St.
Seattle, WA 98119
Phone: 206-378-5536

Seattle (Capitol Hill) # 130
1700 Madison St.
Seattle, WA 98122
Phone: 206-322-7268

Spokane – coming soon!
2975 East 29th Avenue
Spokane, WA 99223
Phone: TBD

University Place # 148
3800 Bridgeport Way West
University Place, WA 98466
Phone: 253-460-2672

Vancouver # 136
305 SE Chkalov Drive #B1
Vancouver, WA 98683
Phone: 360-883-9000

Wisconsin

Glendale # 711
5600 North Port
Washington Road
Glendale, WI 53217
Phone: 414-962-3382

Madison # 712
1810 Monroe Street
Madison, WI 53711
Phone: 608-257-1916

*Although we aim to ensure that the store location information
contained here is correct, we will not be responsible for any
errors or omissions.*

Other titles in this cookbook series:

Cooking with All Things Trader Joe's
by Deana Gunn & Wona Miniati

ISBN 978-0-9799384-8-1

Cooking with Trader Joe's: Companion
by Deana Gunn & Wona Miniati

ISBN 978-0-9799384-9-8

Cooking with Trader Joe's: Dinner's Done!
by Deana Gunn & Wona Miniati

ISBN 978-0-9799384-3-6

Cooking with Trader Joe's: Pack A Lunch!
by Céline Cossou-Bordes

ISBN 978-0-9799384-5-0

Cooking with Trader Joe's: Lighten Up!
by Susan Greeley, MS, RD

ISBN 978-0-9799384-6-7

Available everywhere books are sold.
Please visit us at

CookTJ.com